How I Built a $37 Million
Insurance Agency
in Less Than 7 Years

How I Built a $37 Million Insurance Agency
in Less Than 7 Years

Darren Sugiyama

Hardback ISBN: 978-0-557-63396-8

Paperback ISBN: 978-0-557-94881-9

Contents

Foreword

Providing Clarity

There are so many different types of people that I've worked with over the years. Some of them have been extremely driven ... and some have been extremely lazy. Some have a do-whatever-it-takes attitude, and some have an excuse for everything. Some have been people of their word, and some live their lives based on situational ethics.

One thing I've found in my business life—as well as in my personal life—is that there are some things you can teach people and some things you cannot teach people. Integrity, honesty, character, work ethic, and humility are things of the heart, and things of the heart cannot be taught. These valuable qualities are just part of who that person is. Believe me, I've tried to change people, attempting to motivate them to be more ambitious, more driven, more honest, and I have failed miserably each and every time. That's one of the biggest misconceptions about great leaders.

A great leader doesn't seek to change people. A great leader doesn't try to motivate people. A great leader doesn't attempt to convince people to change their ways. In my opinion, the definition of a great leader is one who helps people clarify what their actual goals are. A great leader gives their disciples step-by-step, systematic directives on how to accomplish these goals.

I'm not a motivator.

I'm a clarifier.

My job is to provide ultimate clarity to my people.

For my clients, I provide the kind of clarity that makes it easy for them to pull the trigger without hesitation or reservation. My entire goal is to give them such a unique experience—an experience that provides such clarity—that they cannot think of *any* reason why they wouldn't want to work with me.

Not one.

When I do this, everyone wins, especially my clients.

When dealing with my employees as their leader, my goal is to provide the kind of clarity that makes it easy for them to execute tasks with precision. They need the kind of clarity that never leaves them confused, wondering what they should do next. They need the kind of clarity and certainty that makes them never want to work for another employer.

This clarity creates an environment based on trust, full disclosure, and mentorship. That's why my employees are both successful and loyal to me.

I provide them with clarity.

So why am I sharing all of these things with you?

I truly believe that my job is to provide you with the same ultimate clarity that my clients have, the same ultimate clarity that my employees have.

This is the ultimate clarity that you're lacking in your business right now.

In business, clarity answers two very important questions:

1.   What *exactly* should I do right now?

2.   How *exactly* should I do it?

This book is the very beginning of your personal journey toward discovering the answers to these two important questions.

The answer to these two questions will prove to be the foundation of your business success. Without them, you will live the rest of your business life feeling frustrated over 80 percent of the time, and in my opinion, that's no way to live.

Once you know exactly what to do and exactly how to do it, things become easy to do. Personally speaking, when I don't know how to do something, I get confused.

When I get confused, I get frustrated.

When I get frustrated, I feel overwhelmed.

When I feel overwhelmed, I freeze up.

Now, you don't have to be a genius or have a Ph.D. in human psychology to know that frustrated, overwhelmed people don't perform very well.

They don't perform well in sports.

They don't perform well in social settings.

And they sure as heck don't perform well in business.

Here's an example of what I mean:

My wife and I recently had our first baby boy, Estevan Kane Sugiyama. When Estevan was born, our friends and family showered him with gifts.

To give you perspective on how many gifts I'm talking about, my wife, Emilia, had four separate baby showers. We got duplicate sets of just about everything. We are very blessed to have so many people in our lives that love us.

That's the good news.

The bad news was that someone had to assemble all of these toys, and unfortunately, that someone was me.

The first box I opened was a baby bouncer. It was a relatively simple apparatus: only about seven parts with a baggy filled with a few nuts and bolts. This was not a complex apparatus, so I figured the assembly would be relatively easy.

Oh, was I wrong.

The first thing I did was open the pamphlet with the assembly instructions in them. They were so confusing that I seriously thought that the manufacturer had made a mistake and put the wrong instructions in with the product.

When I realized the model number on the instructions matched up with the model number on the box, I thought to myself, "Who's the idiot that wrote these crappy instructions?"

I was confused.

I was frustrated.

I froze up.

I just sat there and stared at these stupid instructions for about ten minutes, then crumpled them up, threw them across the room, and yelled out several obscenities.

Frustrated and downright angry, I decided to attempt to figure this out on my own by looking at the picture of the fully-assembled baby bouncer on the box.

What should have only taken me fifteen minutes to assemble took me over an hour, and I was not a happy camper. The instructions were terrible, and thus I was left to figure it out on my own.

Now, think about your business.

Think about how you recruit and train new employees.

Are they having a frustrating baby bouncer assembly experience?

You may say no, but think about this question before you answer it.

Remember my definition of clarity?

In business, clarity answers two very important questions:

1. What *exactly* should I do right now?

2. How *exactly* should I do it?

Do your sales producers know exactly what to say to a prospect to book an appointment?

Now, when I say, exactly, I mean *exactly*.

Do they have a word-for-word verbatim script that has been *proven* to book appointments, and do you have the statistical data reports to back it up?

Do they know what the target booking percentage has *proven* to be over time?

Do they know *exactly* how to read the script? Are they taught about speech inflection—which words to emphasize and where the pregnant pauses should be?

Are they taught the psychology behind every piece of the script?

Are they taught how to break the prospect's current emotional state and how to transition them into the appropriate emotional state to increase the booking percentage through specific words and phrases embedded in the script that communicate to the subconscious mind of the prospect?

Once they book the appointment, have you given them a step-by-step process to confirm that appointment?

Is there a step-by-step process to execute that appointment?

Do they know exactly what to say in that first appointment? Is it scripted?

Are they taught how to use B.I.T.™ Communication Techniques? In other words, do they have specific, step-by-step chronology of benefits, inside stories, and testimonials embedded in that first appointment script?

Oh, I haven't even scratched the surface yet.

If you don't have these specific, premeditated processes dialed in with every employee at your company, then you don't have a system.

If there is no *system*, then there is going to be a lack of clarity.

And what happens when people—human beings—have a lack of clarity?

They get frustrated.

They get overwhelmed.

They freeze up.

Now, should your people be able to figure it out on their own?

Maybe, but they won't. They'll give up.

You may be right in that they *should* be able to figure it out, but it doesn't matter.

What they *should* do is irrelevant.

You may be thinking, "Geez, do I have to show them how to do every little thing, even things that are so obvious?"

The answer, if you want to be incredibly successful in business, is *yes*.

This can be very frustrating for you in the beginning because creating step-by-step, dummy-proof systems that are truly dummy proof is not easy.

It takes a huge amount of work, vision, anticipatory thinking, and time. But the beautiful thing is that once it's done, it's done, and your stress level will get cut in half once a great system is implemented.

Once a great system is running things (and it should run about 80–90 percent of your entire business), *you* don't have to baby sit your business like you are right now.

The system does the babysitting for you, but *only* if you design it properly with clear directives that give your people ultimate clarity.

This is what I do for my consulting clients. My clients hire me to design business systems for their companies that range from billion-dollar corporations all the way down to startup insurance agencies. I design a top-to-bottom system, custom-built for their specific business.

So let's take a quick reality check.

Be honest with yourself.

If you're the boss, are your employees having a frustrating baby bouncer assembly experience because they've never been given such detailed, specific directives?

And what about you?

Are *you* having a frustrating baby bouncer assembly experience in your own business life because you don't have a systematized approach to execute your own tasks?

If you're an independent agent, are *you* having a frustrating baby bouncer assembly experience because the parent company you represent has never given you a simple, step-by-step system to follow, one that has given you ultimate clarity?

I think we both know the answers to these questions.

Don't feel bad.

Outside of McDonalds and Starbucks (and a small handful of other companies, including my own companies), I've never seen a *System-Driven Business* that functions in the way I'm describing.

The goal is to get your business dialed in with these systems I'm talking about so that instead of trying to invent the wheel while your wagon is moving (and about to crash), you can spend more time enjoying the ride while your business system chauffeurs you around. That's why you started your agency in the first place, right?

Yes, you'll make millions of dollars above and beyond your wildest dreams by implementing these systems, but that's not the only reason you want to do this.

The main reason having a *System-Driven Business* is so valuable is it allows you to enjoy your own life, not having every little thing fall on your shoulders.

Build the system, and the system will build the company instead of you having to do everything all by yourself.

So, with that said, let the fun begin. Welcome to my world:

The world of the *System-Driven Business*.

Chapter 1

No Money, Big Vision, and Big Dreams

No Money

I think a lot of people look at me and the companies I've built think that I started out with some sort of special advantage.

If anything, it was just the opposite.

It absolutely makes me cringe when I hear people say, "You have to have money to make money." That's the biggest crock of crap I've ever heard.

That's what broke people say when they're too *chicken* to put their butt on the line and really go for it.

When I first started out, I was broke.

Yes, I was driving a Mercedes, but don't be impressed.

It was a twelve-year-old 190E that had over 109,000 miles on it. The dashboard was all cracked up from the sun, and the black carpet in the back window was so faded that it took on a greenish-brown tone.

One day it died on me, so I took it to the repair shop. The repair guy told me that it was going to cost $3,500 to fix it, but the car was worth less than the cost of repairing it. I ended up selling it to a junkyard for $900.

So there I was with no car and no money to buy a new one.

A friend of mine loaned me his extra car, a Saab convertible.

Again, don't be impressed. It was thirteen years old.

The week after I started driving it, the clutch went out, and I had to cough up $550 on my credit card to get it fixed.

There were rusted out dents running along the passenger side of the car, so I went to the local home improvement store and bought cheap, black rubber mats, the kind they lay down on kitchen floors so you don't slip when you're walking, and I glued them to the side of the car to cover up the rusted-out dents.

To make things worse, this car broke down in front of my new girlfriend's house in Pasadena around one o'clock in the morning, and I had to use her AAA membership card to tow my car back to Huntington Beach, which was about an hour away.

Great way to impress a new girlfriend.

She was a runway supermodel, and she was used to dating all these big-money Hollywood-type guys. Here I was, with a busted up car and no money. At that time, I was basically living off of credit cards. But hey, that's what every aspiring entrepreneur does in the beginning when they're trying to get their business going. It comes with the territory.

Most of my friends lived in Los Angeles, whereas I was living in Orange County.

On the weekends, I'd drive up to LA and join them for dinner and drinks. Of course, I was broke, so I'd eat at home before I joined them, and I'd just order water because it was free.

At the end of the night, sometimes I'd stay at my friend Tommy's place. He had a studio apartment on the outskirts of Beverly Hills, and he usually stayed at his girlfriend Janine's place on the weekends. He gave me a key to his place, so I'd often crash there.

But sometimes, Janine would stay at Tommy's, which meant that I didn't have a place to crash. So, I'd drive into the richest neighborhood I could find in Beverly Hills, pull my car under a tree, and sleep in my car.

It was cold during the winter time, so I'd sleep in this big, puffy ski jacket, two pairs of socks, and two pairs of sweat pants. The next day, I'd wake up and walk into the local gym to take a shower, brush my teeth, and head off to my *satellite office*.

Again, don't be too impressed that I had a *satellite office*. Tommy and I used to have this inside joke about my *satellite office*, which was a coffee shop on the corner of Robertson Boulevard and Beverly Boulevard, right up the street from his apartment.

Most of my Sundays would be spent on my laptop computer at the coffee shop, working on writing new sales scripts, developing marketing ideas, and coming up with new recruiting strategies.

I'd be there from sunup to sundown, working, developing, creating.

I also didn't have a real office yet because I couldn't afford one.

So, my *satellite office* was the coffee shop in Beverly Hills, and my *main office* was the lobby of a luxury hotel in Newport Beach. It felt rich, luxurious, and of course, it was free.

I'd park my car across the street at the mall and walk over to the hotel because I couldn't afford the valet parking.

I'd walk into the lobby wearing my suit and tie, carrying my briefcase. The people at the front desk probably thought I was some successful businessman staying at the hotel. Little did they know I was flat broke, using their lobby as my office.

I used this luxury hotel lobby to do my recruiting interviews, my sales trainings, and my staff meetings.

It was accessible.

It was luxurious.

And it was free.

Big Vision

I had no money, but I had big vision.

If you've ever heard the expression "Act as if …," that was me, acting as if I was this big time insurance tycoon, when in actuality, I was flat broke.

In addition to being broke, the other challenge for me during this time was that I was in the process of developing a system because I didn't have one yet. There was no Darren Sugiyama out there to help me develop one.

So, guess what happens when you try to develop a system from scratch?

You go through a lot of trial and error … emphasis on error.

I tried all kinds of different strategies to generate business.

I signed joint ventures with financial services firms.

I set up referral programs with life insurance agencies.

I joined forces with payroll companies.

On paper, it all looked great. The problem was that none of these joint ventures generated any real business.

I finally said, "Forget all this affinity partnership crap. Let's just get on the phones and start cold calling."

I went out and talked a high-rise building manager into leasing us some office space. It was on the ninth floor of a Class-A office building with a killer view of Newport Beach.

I couldn't afford the office rent at the time, but I borrowed enough money to float me for twelve months. At this point, it was do or die.

I installed the desks and the phones myself over the weekend.

The desks were cheapo $100 desks, and the phones were cheapo $25 phones.

I had a power screw gun, some duct tape, and a whole lot of ambition.

I brought my producers in on Monday and communicated to them my master plan: to take over the world, one insurance policy at a time.

It was time to blaze the phones and book appointments in a way that no one in our industry was doing.

Initially, my people resisted.

I just couldn't get my producers to pick up the phone and dial. I thought I had created a great script, but no one wanted to use it.

Why?

Because most people have an aversion to cold-calling. It doesn't feel professional.

I even had some of my producers tell me, "I didn't come to work for you to be a telemarketer." Even though I talked about the bigger picture, they still didn't want to cold call.

Basically, their egos got in the way.

Then, things got worse. One of my new people had a website that he used to market vacation trips to Baja California, and he posted a Save Money On Health Insurance advertisement on his website. Of course, he had to show everyone in my office, and before I knew it, everyone was coming to me wanting a damn website.

I even had one of my producers meet another broker that claimed they were getting rich selling Individual & Family health insurance plans by nailing *Save Money On Your Health Insurance* signs into telephone poles on busy streets.

Of course, my producer listened to this guy instead of me, so she went out on the weekends and banged signs into telephone polls, even though I advised her not to do it.

Eventually, she got one-too-many blood blisters from hammering her own thumb too many times, and she gave up on the telephone pole advertising idea.

Here I had this great prospecting script, but no one would use it … until this kid named Scott got some results.

Scott was right out of college with no sales experience. In fact, on Scott's first day, I trained him personally, along with three other brand-new producers. I reviewed the script with him and the other producers and told them to start calling, then left the conference room.

Years later, Scott confessed to me that it took him and the three other new producers over twenty minutes to pick up the phone and make the first dial.

Why did it take him so long?

Because Scott is a human being, just like everybody else.

People fear the unknown.

The difference between successful people and unsuccessful people is that successful people take action despite their fear of the unknown.

So Scott started dialing.

And he dialed some more.

And he dialed some more.

By his third year working with me, he topped over $100,000 in income.

Today, he's been with me for over six years and is now my right-hand man as the *Director of New Producer Development* at my firm. He lives in a million dollar penthouse, two blocks from the beach, and drives a $93,000 Mercedes. Not bad for a thirty-one-year-old.

I first told Scott that it would take some time to get his commissions built up, but if he stuck with me long enough, he'd develop an incredible career with me. He believed in my vision, and that's exactly what happened.

From the very beginning, Scott identified himself to me as a potential leader, but I had to teach him about leadership and the importance of building a company culture.

Building a company culture is one of the most important things in building a super agency—or any business, for that matter.

Your people have to want to be part of something bigger than themselves, and that type of team mindset is only developed through developing a company culture.

A strong company culture defines many things:

It defines your company's value system.

It defines your company's mission and identity.

It defines your company's brand.

Your company culture dictates how your people think, how they walk, how they talk, how they operate, and even what clothing they wear.

A strong company culture has rules, and these rules must be established from the very beginning.

I told Scott that if he wanted to be my right-hand man, he had to operate just like me.

When we walked to the copy machine, we walked fast.

When we talked on the phone, we talked loud.

We wore navy blue pin-striped suits, crisp white shirts, and bright red power ties.

We were always talking about building a dynasty, a super agency that our industry had never seen before.

Scott wanted in.

We zeroed in on a specific demographic and started recruiting people that were the right fit for our company culture.

I was on to something big, and Scott knew it.

Big Dreams

Shortly thereafter, I found George.

George was an ex-professional basketball player from Bulgaria who knew someone that knew someone that knew me. I interviewed George at a coffee shop in Beverly Hills.

What impressed me most about George was that he was so hungry to learn.

He didn't have much talent when he started out with me, but his work ethic was tremendous.

He and Scott eventually helped me lead the charge.

I'd get into the office at 6:30 AM, before anyone got there.

Scott and George would come in at 8:00 AM on the dot, sometimes a bit earlier.

Most of my producers at that time would stroll in around 9:00 AM and some at 10:00 AM, but that wasn't the culture I was trying to build. I wanted an environment where we always got a head start on our competition.

At the end of the day, most of our people left the office around 5:00 PM or 6:00 PM, but Scott and George kept working with me up until about 9:00 PM and sometimes stayed until 10:00 PM.

In most high-rise buildings, they turn the air conditioning off toward the end of the day, so at night, my office got extremely hot. Once Scott and George left for the day, I'd barricade the door with a couple of chairs, take off my suit and tie, including my pants, and work bare-chested in my boxer shorts until midnight, sometimes until 1:00 AM.

On the drive home from the office, in the middle of the night, I would have conversations with myself.

I was working fifteen to sixteen-hour days, seven days a week. I'd keep the same routine, even on Saturdays and Sundays.

At this point, my weekend trips up to my *satellite office* in Beverly Hills were over. I practically lived in my office.

A girl I was dating at the time would meet me in my office on Saturday night, usually bringing me dinner, because I just never took a break.

We'd have dinner (among other things) on the conference room table, and that was pretty much the extent of my dating life at that time.

I was focused and driven, and nothing was going to get in the way of my success.

It was now September 2003, and despite my obsessive work schedule, I didn't have much to show for my efforts. This insurance industry was something new to me, and I was trying to figure it out as I went along.

At this point, the total gross revenue to my firm totaled a whopping $287 per month, and that was before I paid out commission splits to my producers.

Yes, you heard that number correctly.

My entire firm was only generating $287 per month. My office overhead in that small office was over $7,000 per month including office rent, our receptionist's salary, and basic business expenses. I was going deeper and deeper in debt.

When I say I was frustrated, you have no idea just how frustrated I was.

I was running out of credit on my credit cards.

I had sold my childhood baseball card collection to pay rent one month.

I sold my surfboard and my mountain bike to pay rent the next month.

I remember one Saturday night, I drove up to Santa Monica to hang out with some friends, something that I hadn't done in months. Some friends of mine told me about this hot new club, so I met them there.

As I walked through the club, the music was hot.

The girls there were hot.

The place was on fire.

But you know that feeling when you know you don't deserve to enjoy yourself because you feel like you haven't earned the right to enjoy yourself yet?

Well, that's how I felt.

I thought to myself, "Man, I've got no reason to celebrate. My business isn't growing. I'm dead broke. I don't even know if I'm ever going to be successful at this shit."

I think a lot of people that didn't know me back then don't believe me when I talk about this beginning stage of my career. They can't imagine me being depressed about business because they only see my business for what it is today.

They can't imagine me lacking confidence because they only see the ultra-confident, polished version of Darren Sugiyama today.

What they don't realize is that they're only seeing the finished, polished product, but there was once a time when I was a broke, struggling, wannabe entrepreneur, and I certainly wasn't polished.

That night, after walking around the bar for just ten minutes, I just walked out.

I spent the rest of the night wandering the streets of Santa Monica by myself, thinking about everything.

I thought about all of the business models I'd tried.

I thought about all the dreams I had and the hunger I had in my belly to be successful in business.

I thought about all the blood, sweat, and tears I had put into trying to build my empire.

And I thought about how broke I was and the lack of results that I had produced thus far.

I felt like such a failure.

Nobody knew it.

My family didn't know it.

My friends didn't know it.

And I sure as hell didn't let Scott and George know it.

It's one thing to feel like a loser because you haven't reached the level of success you've always wanted to reach, but it's another thing to shoulder the burden of promising other people that you would lead them to the Promised Land with you and doubting whether or not you have the ability to do so.

That's the burden that a leader accepts.

That's the burden that a great leader embraces.

And so that was the promise that I made to Scott and George, as well as anyone else that was willing to put their faith in me.

They say that you can tell a lot about a man based on the size of his dreams.

I certainly had visions of grandeur, and my dreams were bigger than life itself.

But they also say that you can tell the size of a man's dream based on the size of the things that can steal it.

I've seen so many people give up on their dreams because of their circumstances.

Maybe it was a group of negative friends that talked them out of pursuing their dreams.

Maybe it was a negative family member that made them doubt their own abilities.

Maybe it was a negative spouse that nagged them or repeatedly put them down.

Maybe it was an immediate financial challenge and a lack of ingenuity to make ends meet as they were pursuing their dream.

Maybe it was a setback or two that made them give up.

Whatever the reasons (some people call them reasons, whereas I call them weak-ass excuses), these people have basically rationalized that their excuse was bigger than their dream.

Well, my dreams were *big*, bigger than any stupid little setback or adversity I could ever endure, and believe me, I had many setbacks and faced many adversities.

I made the commitment that I wasn't going to let anyone or anything stop me.

I wasn't going to let anyone or anything steal my dream.

So, there I was. Broke financially and on the verge of breaking spiritually, but giving up was just not an option. That's what wusses do, and I ain't no wuss.

In October 2003, I had a major breakthrough.

Several key components of what I now call a *System-Driven Business* came together. There were three main components that proved to be the foundation of our newly found success.

Key Component #1:

The first key component was our ability to recruit producers.

When I first started out, everyone told me that it was impossible to recruit people on straight commission with no base salary.

This was during a time when the job market was booming.

College graduates with no experience were getting jobs with starting salaries of up to $40,000.

The mortgage refinance industry was on fire, and out here in Newport Beach, California, there were tons of kids in their twenties doing re-fi's and making $250,000 a year.

They were driving Lamborghinis, living like rock stars, and dropping $2,000 a night for a VIP table at the nightclubs.

Even though I knew that industry wasn't sustainable long-term, try telling that to a twenty-four-year old making $250,000 a year. They just didn't believe me.

Or even worse, try telling that to your producers working on straight commission (who aren't rich yet) that have friends making that kind of money. In our business, it takes several months to ramp up, and at the beginning of a producer's career, it's a bit of a financial struggle.

I had to compete in a job market that made my opportunity look second-rate.

So how did I overcome that?

I had to find people that believed in the bigger picture dream I was pitching.

It was the dream of building something long-term, a foundation that would last them the rest of their lives.

I also focused on building an organization that felt like one-third powerful corporation, one-third family, and one-third championship sports team.

I knew that we needed to find people that wanted to be financially successful, but more importantly, we needed people that wanted to be part of something special, something bigger than themselves.

We focused on developing a culture of people that truly wanted to help our clients, and we made no apologies for pointing out all of the wrongdoings other brokers were committing against their clients.

It wasn't like it was a difficult thing to do.

So many brokers kept their clients in the dark regarding creative ways to reduce the cost of their insurance premiums.

There were only two reasons why other brokers were doing this:

One, they didn't have the knowledge of how to strategically formulate a better employee benefits package using new tax codes and new consumer-driven health plans, thus resulting in the client overpaying for limited benefits.

Or two, they *did* have the capacity to save their clients money but elected to *not* show them lower cost options because they wanted to maximize their commissions at the expense of their client's budget.

These unscrupulous and untalented brokers were making hundreds of thousands of dollars by keeping their clients in the dark.

I quickly realized that if that's what the majority of brokers were doing, then all we had to do was expose these wrongdoings to these clients and show them their true options.

All we had to do was vigilantly help clients by showing them better options and better-engineered strategies.

Key Component #2:

The second key component was the refinement of our cold-calling script.

We refined our script to the point where we knew exactly how many appointments our script would book per week based on quantifiable statistics.

Virtually everyone we put on the phones with this magical script booked the same amount of appointments.

Once we perfected this process, we were halfway there.

We had so many appointments, so many sales opportunities that we went from feeling like desperate sales people, begging for the deal, to feeling like rock stars and our prospects started begging *us* to help *them*.

It was a total paradigm shift and a lot more fun, quite frankly.

I was personally running twenty to twenty-five sales appointments per week.

The confidence and swagger that comes with an abundance of sales opportunities (nonexistent when you have a scarcity of sales opportunities) was in full effect.

Finally, things were really coming together.

Key Component #3:

The third key component was our ability to build a culture.

We had six producers that said they wanted to be part of our culture.

My original core crew wasn't perfect by any means.

Of the six, two of them turned out to be absolute nightmares, and one of them, though a really nice guy, just didn't put in the effort required to be successful.

However, the other three really took off like rocket ships, and those three producers are still with me today, all doing *very* well, all making more money than most doctors make. This was the beginning of establishing a true culture.

In order to build a company culture, you've got to have one person leading the charge in your organization, and that person is usually going to be you, initially.

If you can find one person to buy into your vision, your values, your belief system, and your standard method of operation, then you've got a co-leader. If you and that co-leader can just get one more producer to buy into these beliefs, you've got a culture. All you need are three strong members subscribing to your culture because at that point, every new person you bring into your organization will assimilate into your culture, and now you've got momentum.

So the one-two-three punch was:

1.   Recruit good people that wanted to work hard.

2.   Train them to read the script.

3.   Build our culture.

We suffered a miserable start in 2003, our first year of business.

In that year, we made a whopping $592.73, and that's before I paid the commission splits out to my producers.

Yes, you heard that number correctly. We made less than $600 in total commissions for the entire year.

But remember what I said. In October of 2003, we started to gain momentum.

Just twelve months later in 2004, we made $370,685.67.

In 2005, we took quantum leaps.

My gross commissions for 2005 totaled over $1.3 million.

That year, my December commissions alone totaled $167,643.74 per month, which was a run-rate of over $2 million in annual commissions. We basically went from zero to over $2 million a year in commissions in twenty-four months. From there, things continued to grow in leaps and bounds, and the rest is history.

Here we are in 2010, and I'm blessed to say that my agency is larger and more successful than I would have ever dreamed. We just did $37 million in premiums last year, which was our seventh year in business.

Out of forty thousand brokers in the state of California, we're consistently in the top thirty with almost every insurance carrier. We've been the number one producing agency in the nation with Health Net, number twenty-two in California with Blue Cross, number one in Orange County with Blue Shield, number two in California with Aetna, number one in the nation with Colonial Life, number one in Southern California with Kaiser Permanente, and the list goes on.

In fact, Kaiser Permanente even took me to the 2008 Olympics in Beijing. To give you an idea of how exclusive this was, they only took me and two other brokers on this trip. We sat in the third row at the closing ceremonies. To give you an idea of how exclusive these seats were, Vince Vaughn (the movie star from *Wedding Crashers* and *Fred Claus*) was sitting fifteen rows behind me. Imagine that. I had better seats at the Olympics than a movie star. Believe me, that put a big smile on my face.

So, people ask me all the time, "How did you do it? How did you build such a successful business in such a short amount of time?"

In this book, I'm going to share with you some of my most valuable secrets of how I did it and how I'm still doing it.

This will be the best book you've ever read regarding how to build your empire.

Chapter 2

How to Become a Master Recruiter

Becoming a Master Recruiter

First and foremost, being a Master Recruiter doesn't mean that your goal is to contract as many people as you can, talking as many people as you can into your opportunity.

A Master Recruiter identifies the right candidates that are the right fit for their organization. I can't tell you how many people I've talked to in the insurance industry (as well as other industries) that self-admittedly do a sleazy bait-and-switch in the interview process.

I even know a managing director of a very well-known life insurance company that blatantly lies about how much money he makes to his recruits.

How do I know this?

Because one of my best friends that I grew up with was a co-groomsman in a mutual friend's wedding party with this sleaze ball. He told me that this guy was bragging about how he tells recruits that he makes more than triple the income he actually makes.

When my friend asked him, "How can you lie like that?" this guy replied, "Hey, I'll tell them *anything* to rope them in."

Unbelievable. I hate liars more than I hate anything in life.

I'll say that again. I *hate* liars.

Liars have to lie because they're too weak and untalented to win on their own merit. Liars are total wusses.

Plus, in the insurance industry, there's so much opportunity that there's no need to lie. There isn't even a need to embellish the truth. Just tell them the truth. Not only is it the right thing to do ethically, but there is so much opportunity to become wealthy in the insurance industry that lying is unnecessary.

A Master Recruiter also understands that it's a waste of time to try to convince someone to enter into a career in the insurance industry. It's obvious that people make hundreds of thousands of dollars (and sometimes millions) in the insurance game. There's no need to convince anyone to do anything.

You're looking for driven people that understand that they can make a much larger income on straight commission (because it's performance-based) rather than taking a cubicle job with a cruddy base salary.

Focus on communicating to your target demographic throughout the entire recruiting process. You'll turn off over 80 percent of the interview candidates, but that's exactly what you want to do. Those people would have never survived on straight commission because they aren't performers. They're cubicle workers.

You want your entire message to be focused on providing clarity for the 20 percent that want a big-time opportunity. Of this 20 percent, half of them will realize that they don't have the guts to go for it, and their fear will dominate their decision, in which case they'll remove themselves from the interview process.

This leaves you with the remaining 10 percent.

This 10 percent wants something more out of their career.

They don't want to settle for the Good Life; they want the Great Life.

Still, just because someone wants the Great Life doesn't mean they're willing to do what it takes to get it. They believe in their heart of hearts that they're willing to pay their dues and sacrifice in the beginning to achieve the Big Time. They'll tell you they're smart enough to realize that it doesn't happen overnight and that in order to truly capitalize on any great opportunity, there will be hard work involved, obsessive work involved.

Of this 10 percent, half of them are just big talkers. We call them ATNAs: All Talk, No Action. You have to expect this or you'll be setting yourself up for disappointment. These people will tell you how this is the perfect career for them and how they don't understand why everyone doesn't do this. They'll tell you how amazed they are that other people just don't get it. They'll tell you everything you want to hear, and if you're gullible, you'll buy into their rhetoric—hook, line, and sinker—and then when they do nothing, you'll be heartbroken.

Perhaps you've already experienced this.

Don't fall for the big talkers. Talk is cheap. Look for action.

The action will come from the remaining 5 percent. This is the 5 percent that you want to target. This 5 percent appreciates bluntness and directness.

They don't want to hear the fluff, and they can sniff out fluff and hype from the very beginning.

If you just shoot straight with these people, provide them clarity as to what they'll be doing and how they'll be doing it, and give them very specific statistical data of how your *System-Driven Business* operates and how you quantify performance results, this 5 percent will beg you to bring them on your team.

The other 95 percent of the people that you interview just aren't cut out for this. You'd be wasting your time (and theirs) if you tried to convince them to join your team.

Always remember: recruiting isn't about contracting the most interviewees. It's about contracting the right interviewees. The Master Recruiter interviews as many candidates as possible in search of the right players that fall into that 5 percent niche and *only* contracts them.

Let's do the numbers.

Out of every twenty interviewees, 80 percent of them won't be interested after the first interview because they know they wouldn't do what it takes to be successful in our industry. They'll voluntarily remove themselves from the interview process. That means only four of them will come back for a second interview.

Of the four, half of them will realize that even though they were excited about the opportunity, they're emotionally weak, and they'll come up with an excuse as to why they just can't work on straight commission.

Of the two that are left standing, one of them will tell you how perfect they are for this type of opportunity and how they'll do whatever it takes to be successful. Whenever someone tells you that they'll do whatever it takes to be successful, run for the hills.

Everyone that has ever told me this was a self-indulgent, lazy liar.

It's like a boyfriend or a girlfriend that tells you, "I would never cheat on you." They're basically telling you that because it's just the opposite, and they probably have a track record of cheating on past girlfriends or boyfriends.

In business, when someone says, "I would never screw anybody over for money," it's because that's exactly what they'd do, and they've probably done it before, so don't believe the person that tells you how hard they're willing to work or how they'll do whatever it takes.

Look for the person that has a proven track record of working hard and doing whatever it takes. The person that put him or herself through school, working two or three jobs, the person that was a successful college athlete, the person that was the president or chairperson of their fraternity or sorority, the person that has grinded it out in some other capacity—*these* are the type of people you want to recruit into your agency.

It's not about contracting the most candidates; it's about interviewing the most candidates and contracting the right candidates.

It all starts with your job postings.

Job Postings

Your job posting must be *unique*.

It must be written in a way that *jumps* off the page, differentiating it from all of the other job postings. The majority of job postings are boring and, quite frankly, they all sound the same.

They talk about company revenues, when the company was established, what their A.M. Best rating is, blah, blah, blah. None of these things make the job searcher curious to find out more.

There is usually ONE main thing you're looking for in a new-hire candidate. It's the *one* quality that is an absolute must-have in order to succeed in our industry. The job posting should be written to attract *that* type of candidate and *only* that type of candidate. Why would you want to waste your time interviewing someone that wasn't right for the position?

If you're looking for straight-commissioned sales people, your job posting should include in its description very specific things about your corporate culture and your office environment. For example, in my sales job postings, I always include things like, "We work hard and play hard." Another great line to use in your job posting is, "If you want a career with no glass ceiling, this may be the opportunity for you."

These things don't sound professional, but they do sound compelling, which is your entire goal.

You should also have a link to your website on the job posting. Now, that being said, it's under the assumption that your website is compelling. The problem is that most websites suck.

They're littered with tons of boring jargon. Let me put it this way: if you can imagine Dan Rather reading the content on your website, then your website sucks.

Your website should be clean and easy to navigate.

When it comes to effectively communicating on a website (especially for the purposes of recruiting), less is more when it comes to text.

Websites that are loaded with video testimonials do a much better job communicating your message, mainly because you're getting third-party validation. Plus, it's a format that very few websites are taking advantage of, which differentiates your company from the rest.

If you look at my website, it's loaded with videos, with very little text. For whatever reason, people are conditioned to watch videos/TV/movies as their primary source of information and entertainment. People are also conditioned to believe that the information viewed on a screen/TV/monitor is more credible than any other source.

Why is that?

I have no idea, but it's a fact.

Think about the last time you flew in an airplane. Sometimes, the flight attendants will do a seatbelt/oxygen mask demonstration while standing in the aisle just prior to take-off, and *no one* pays any attention to them. However, when that same information is communicated on a video monitor, more than half of the people watch the stupid video.

If you haven't figured this out yet, I'm a big fan of videos on websites. Videos create an experience for the viewer as opposed to just giving them facts and statistics about your company.

With your website, you're trying to create a unique *experience* for your candidates (as well as your prospects and clients). They should look at your website and your videos and say to themselves, "Wow, these guys are different. I want to meet them."

Again, video testimonials are *huge* in building your agency's credibility. It's that third-party validation that is so valuable. When you have third-party validation, you don't have to toot your own horn. It's always much more effective to have other people toot your horn for you, plus it comes off much less narcissistic (not that I have a problem with narcissism).

However, when your image becomes self-indulgent and you're perceived as being a braggart, the effect is lost. Third-party validation through video testimonials is the most powerful way to accomplish this shameless self-promotion without appearing self-indulgent.

I always author the job postings for my clients that hire me for business development consulting. My goal is to give them an incredibly unique image and brand, and it all starts with how you portray your agency to the interview candidates. Interview candidates always comment on how compelling our job posting was when they come in to interview with us. Again, the posting *only* attracts candidates that want to be obsessive, semi-workaholics: people that are looking for a big opportunity.

Scheduling Interviews

Okay, so you have this incredibly compelling job posting. The question is, what do you do once you begin receiving responses from candidates?

There are three major rules I have when it comes to recruiting producers.

Rule #1: Never talk to a job candidate prior to the interview.

This is the worst thing you can do. The candidate is going to grill you with a million questions. And what is the recruiter going to end up doing? They're going to answer every question as they get grilled.

Now, who's in control: the recruiter or the candidate?

The candidate is.

And the sad thing is that the candidate hasn't even had the firsthand experience of being in the organization's environment yet, so they don't even know what questions to ask. They ask things like, "What's the base salary," or, "How many hours a week do I have to work," or, "Do you offer benefits and health insurance?"

The problem with these questions is that they can't be answered in totality on a five-minute phone call. The candidate needs to see the whole picture before you allow them to make assumptions about your opportunity.

That's why I never talk to a candidate prior to the in-person interview. I *only* want them to experience my company under *my* conditions, in *my* format, on *my* terms.

Again, that's what the videos on my website are for. If the videos on your website are compelling enough, the candidate will play by your rules unless you allow them to control the process, which is a big mistake.

So here's the process:

My assistant receives e-mails from candidates that are responding to the online job posting. If the candidate calls my office wanting information, they are directed to e-mail my assistant. If they insist on talking to someone, then we take away the opportunity from them. We *only* operate on our terms when it comes to this process.

Why am I so adamant about this?

Because I've allowed candidates to control the process in the past, back when I was an Amateur Recruiter, and it *never* panned out well. Not once.

Not once.

Rule #2: Never meet with an interviewee one-on-one for a first interview.

I *only* do group interviews for first interviews.

The reason is that I have no idea whether I'm going to like the interviewee prior to the interview. A résumé can only tell you so much about the candidate. You need to see how they interact and communicate with other people, which the group interview provides.

I used to interview people one-on-one for the first interview, but the problem was that I would block out a full hour for each interviewee. If I didn't like the interviewee, I lost that hour of productive time because I had to wait for the next interviewee to come in an hour later. In a group interview, I never waste time on an unqualified interviewee because I'm meeting with the entire group at one time.

The other problem I experienced was that many of these one-on-one interviewees came in with an attitude, as if *they* were interviewing *me*. I actually felt as though I had to sell them on the opportunity. Now, if you've ever been to any of my trainings, you know that I don't want to try to convince anyone to do anything.

If you're in the convincing game, you're in a position of weakness.

That's what happens in the one-on-one interview unless you interrogate them. If your interview is an interrogation, then you're in control, but the problem is that interrogating someone doesn't make them want to work for you.

The other problem with this approach is that the candidate never gets to learn about why your opportunity is so great because all you did was make them talk about themselves. You need to talk about how great your opportunity is, and *no one* is going to work for you on straight commission unless you give them a compelling reason to.

If you're doing one-on-one interviews on the first interview, you're going to be perceived as the Desperate Convincer, begging them to join you, or as the Interrogator, having no appeal whatsoever to the interviewee.

Neither role is compelling nor attractive.

Neither role will successfully recruit the ideal producer.

Another problem with one-on-one interviews is that about 20–30 percent of the confirmed interviewees never show up. This is a big waste of my time. When I started doing group interviews, I'd schedule ten candidates for the group interview. I knew that of the ten candidates, three of them would no-show. No problem. I now had a group interview with seven candidates, which is exactly what I wanted in the first place. No time wasted.

Perhaps the main reason that I *only* do group interviews for the candidate's first interview is that it's the only way to create the right environment conducive to giving the interviewee the experience that I want him or her to have.

In this group interview, I talk about the industry, I talk about timing, I talk about my producers and how successful they've become, I talk about our systematized approach, I talk about our mentorship and development program, and I talk about the three qualities we look for in interviewees.

The three qualities I'm looking for are:

1. Raw intelligence

2. Work ethic

3. Coachability

These are three qualities that I cannot teach. They are characteristics that I believe are part of the person's DNA. I can't teach someone to be smart. If they're a dumb-dumb, there's really nothing I can do about it.

If they're lazy, they're lazy. Laziness is a character flaw that is part of who that person is. I'll tell candidates right off the bat that if they're not ready to be a semi-workaholic for the next two years to go and take a cubicle job. This type of opportunity isn't for them.

I'll also tell them that if they want to leave the office at 4:59 pm everyday and try to do as little work as possible that they should go take a dead-end cubicle job with a base salary. They'll be much happier.

But if they're going to work hard—simply because that's the kind of person they are—then they should be compensated for that, and in my company, they'll be overcompensated.

My top guys make more than most doctors and attorneys, and logic would tell the interviewees that if they want to make that kind of money, they're going to have to work their butts off.

This brings me to the third quality: coachability.

The recruit must be an excellent student of our system. If the recruit has an over-inflated view of him or herself and they're not willing to take specific directions, then forget it. They'll never make it in my system.

It always cracks me up when a rookie tells me that they want to do it their way.

Give me a break.

I'll tell them:

"I built a $37 million company in less than seven years. Have you ever done that? Listen, sonny boy: you haven't made a dime in this business, and you want to question my system? I've got guys making over $200,000 working for me that had *zero* experience in the insurance industry prior to working for me. You either want to be like one of my guys, or you don't."

I know my system works, so I don't have the time or the patience to work with an uncoachable producer. That's why I try to scrub these people out in the interview process. I'd rather recruit less producers than be stuck with a bunch of uncoachable liabilities.

So that's what I'm looking for—smart people that will work their butts off doing *exactly* what I teach them to do, how I teach them to do it. This is the formula for success in my agency, both for the producers, themselves, and the agency as a whole.

Rule #3: Make the interviewee accommodate *your* schedule, not the other way around.

Once my assistant receives an e-mail inquiry from the candidate, she copies and pastes a pre-authored interview invitation (authored by me, of course) and e-mails the candidate with a specified date and time.

I *only* do group interviews (first interviews) on Tuesdays at 4:00 PM. The day and time is irrelevant, but having *one* time slot you interview in is imperative. If the candidate says their schedule doesn't allow or if they request a different date and time, here's the e-mail template my assistant e-mails them:

"Unfortunately, Mr. Sugiyama's schedule only allows for this particular date and time. If you can rearrange your schedule to fit his, please let me know. Otherwise, we wish you the best of luck in your future endeavors."

Usually, they'll rearrange their schedule.

Every time I've made an exception, I've either gotten burned with a no-show or the candidate was the wrong candidate.

Trust me on this one. Do *not* bend your rules for anyone.

I know this seems very stringent and unaccommodating, but using this rule will save you a lot of time and frustration. Remember, the key to a *System-Driven Business* is to set your rules and not break them. This is part of your SMO (Standard Method Of Operation).

The First Impression

The first impression you make on an interview candidate is incredibly important. I always have interviewees wait a minimum of five minutes in the foyer.

Why? Because I want them to soak in the environment.

I want them to look at our awards, client testimonial letters, and luxury magazines. I want them to get a feel of who we are, reinforcing the image they experienced on our website through our videos.

I also have upbeat music playing at relatively high volumes throughout the office, including the foyer at relatively high volumes. I want to create a high-energy, fun environment. I use iTunes internet radio. Typically, deep house music works the best. If you're not familiar with this type of music, it's basically up-tempo dance music with a strong beat.

The candidates should be waiting in the foyer, anticipating the unknown. This lends to the mystique of our operation. They are then escorted into the conference room for the group interview.

Ideally, there should be four to eight interviewees in a group interview. Any more than eight interviewees starts to feel like a cattle call. Even if many of the confirmed interviewees flake out and no-show (which happens with 20–30 percent of the interview confirmations), it's not a problem. I've done interviews with just two candidates in a group interview, and it's still very effective.

Prior to me stepping into the conference room to begin the group interview, the interviewees watch an eight-minute video about our firm. It's loaded with testimonials of insurance carrier executives talking about my agency as well as some of my producers talking about what it's like to work for me and the success they've achieved with me.

By the time I step into the room, the credibility factor is a nonissue. In fact, the video actually celebritizes me and my producers. The video sets the stage for the group interview.

I produce a customized recruiting video for all of my A-list consulting clients. It revamps their entire image and agency brand; this video brands the agency and the owner.

In addition to creating an agency brand, you also need to create a personal brand. These people are going to be working with you, and as the leader of the agency, your people want to know that they're following someone that's worth following. Your personal brand must be so compelling that your interviewees would die just to be associated with you and learn from you because you've positioned yourself as the mastermind behind your people's massive success. You are the "Magic Man."

Introductions

First off, I have everyone introduce him or herself.

The interviewees give me their name, school they graduated from, and why they specifically wanted to interview with my firm. Typically, the best interviewees recognize what makes my organization unique, and they're able to articulate to me what those things are. They would have learned these things via the videos on our website.

If they didn't watch the videos on my website, it tells me that they're unprepared, which tells me a lot about their lack of attention to detail. This almost disqualifies them right off the bat. I'm looking for the candidate that is presold on my opportunity prior to coming into the interview. I'm also looking to see how the interviewees present themselves when speaking in front of their peers (the other interviewees).

For the remainder of the group interview, I talk about the opportunity. I don't ask them any more questions about themselves. I save that for the second interview, which is done in a one-on-one environment.

The group interview must have the same exact format every single time. It's basically a script. Here are the topics I discuss at a group interview:

The Economy

I start off discussing how most companies are struggling with the current economic conditions, and I explain why we're actually prospering despite the challenge.

I talk about the fact that now more than ever, business owners are open to talking to us about creative ways to save money on their insurance (without sacrificing richness in benefits), and it's all because of the current economic conditions. I highlight the fact that the timing has never been better for them to enter this career with us because of these conditions. It's important for you to highlight the window of opportunity.

It's like the janitor that started working for Microsoft at the right time and took stock options over a Christmas bonus. Today, he's driving a Ferrari. Sometimes, timing is everything.

The Type of Work We Do

I then run through two or three case studies of real clients. I show the interviewees how we helped these clients and what the final outcomes were. Interviewees need to see what type of work they'd be doing. They need to see that we have unique, cutting-edge, semi-proprietary strategies that give us the edge in the marketplace.

This is where your USP (Unique Selling Proposition) comes in. Clients need to know why they should do business with you, and *only* you, and your interviewees need to know why they should work for you and *only* you.

In our organization, the number one reason people come to work for us is our mentorship program. We highlight the fact that they're going to have the opportunity to learn directly from the top producers at our firm—top producers that started out just like them, at ground zero, and worked their way to the top doing *exactly* what they're going to teach them to do.

Our leaders are credible leaders because they have all personally done what they're teaching our new people to do.

Our new producers have more respect for their mentors because they know they started out at ground zero, just like the leaders.

Our leaders have more respect for our new people because they remember what it was like starting out at the bottom, just like the new producers.

This mentorship model is the best training program I've ever seen because it really teaches the new producer every element of the game, hands on. It also helps to ensure the new producer's success because he or she has one of my heavy hitters closing business for him or her in the beginning on a case-split. They not only witness success, but they also experience it first hand.

Scrubbing the Interviewees

I know recruiters that will try to talk interviewees into the opportunity by selling the opportunity too hard. This is a major mistake. The last thing you want to do is talk an interviewee into the opportunity.

Believe me, I'm *very* good at talking people into the opportunity, but when I used to do this (because I didn't know any better at the time), I ended up with a weak producer that I had to resell on the opportunity every week, and ultimately, that producer would end up quitting anyway. Now that I've stopped making this stupid mistake, my producer retention is much higher, and I don't find myself wasting time trying to mentor and train someone that was really never a good fit for my organization in the first place.

I'm looking for people that recognize the opportunity and recognize the fact that they're going to get something special from being a part of my firm. I'm looking for people that truly understand the value of great mentorship.

If they understand this, *they'll* be the ones begging *me* for the opportunity, not the other way around.

This is very similar to what I teach in my sales trainings. I never want to convince a prospect to do business with me. I want to do an excellent job clarifying the advantages of doing business with me (in a systematic, scripted format). When I do this properly, I attract the right type of clients, and they literally *beg* me to help them. This changes the dynamic of the relationship from the very beginning.

Q and A Session

I wrap up the group interview with letting them ask me questions. I'm very direct and blunt about this Q and A session.

The interviewees have now seen the whole picture of who we are and what we do. They can now make a good decision regarding whether or not they think this arrangement is right for them or not.

I love the Q and A session. It clarifies in their minds (as well as in my mind) whether or not they have what it takes to be successful in my organization.

I always end the group interview by bringing in one of my top producers to do Q and A with the interviewees. Interviewees will always trust what one of your top producers says over what you say. In their minds, you're the owner of the agency, so you must have a biased, hidden agenda of trying to talk them into it. Regardless of what you do, they will have this perception. Therefore, bringing in one of your top guys to talk to them (without you in the room) gives you the third-party credibility you need.

The Next Step

I wrap up the session (after one of my top producers has gotten a chance to field their questions for 10 minutes) by telling them that I'm going to e-mail them four questions that revolve around our discussion and that I'll need their answers e-mailed back to me directly by the end of the next day. I obviously have my philosophy about why I ask certain questions in this e-mail.

That being said, you need to identify which specific qualities are the absolute necessary qualities that someone needs to have in order to succeed in your organization and formulate your questions around uncovering whether or not the candidates have these specific qualities.

Here's the genius behind this process:

If they respond by answering my questions, then I book the one-on-one interview. This interviewee was proactive enough to e-mail me with his or her answers, which tells me that he or she is hungry for my opportunity.

I'm looking for the candidates that are trying to sell me on why I should bring them on board. If they're not chasing me down, then they don't want to work with me badly enough to justify me offering them this golden opportunity.

You'll have several interviewees that don't respond at all.

Fantastic.

They disqualified themselves, and you preserved your ego by not putting yourself in the position of weakness, offering them the opportunity just because they had a heartbeat and a social security number.

You only offered them the chance to continue the interview process. You didn't offer them a position yet, so if they remove themselves from the process, you never got rejected.

I *never* follow up with interviewees after I e-mail them the four questions. I'm looking for proactive people that are chasing me for the opportunity.

I chase no one.

I convince no one.

I beg no one.

They need to beg me in order to have the right to work with me. That's my rule, and it has worked out wonderfully ever since I implemented it. Again, one of the reasons my producer retention is so high is that I only bring in people that recognized that working with my firm is an incredibly unique opportunity.

When it comes to effective recruiting, get out of the Convincing Game, and get into the Clarifying Game.

Lastly, you want to make sure you wrap up the interview before the interviewees want to leave. You have to leave them wanting more.

The best way to do this is to constantly look at your watch as you're wrapping things up. When you tell them that they'll receive the four questions via e-mail, tell them that you'll need those answers back before the close of the day tomorrow and that once you review their answers, depending on their answers, you may invite them back for a second one-on-one interview.

Once you tell them this, you should walk out of the room immediately. Don't hang around and schmooze. You'll lose power if you do this.

Here's another important post-interview tip: never thank an interviewee for coming to an interview. *They* should be thanking *you* for the opportunity. When you thank them for coming in, subconsciously, they'll see you as a desperate convincer that is sucking up to them, trying to get them to join you.

You want the exact opposite to happen. They should be trying to convince you to take them on. In this book, I'll be talking a lot about changing the dynamic of interaction between you and your interviewees as well as changing the dynamic of the relationship between you and your client.

Chapter 3

People-Driven vs. System-Driven

People-Driven vs. System-Driven

As you can imagine, I've seen the inside operations of a lot of businesses.

Whether it's a client I'm doing business development consulting for or a company I'm considering doing business with, practically every single one of these companies is not System-Driven.

They're People-Driven.

What I mean by this is that the success (or failure) of these companies is completely in the hands of the employees, based on their knowledge, skill, contacts, relationships, intelligence, and human abilities.

Having talented employees is great. Don't get me wrong.

But the problem with this people-driven, talent-driven model is multifold, especially in an insurance agency.

Let's start out talking about the recruiting process and the demographics of your new-hire candidates.

Most agencies try to recruit producers with experience because they perceive that training a new producer is going to be too much work.

Here's the problem with this approach:

If you recruit based on talent and experience, you've got to ask yourself, "If this guy is already such a great producer, why does he want to come and work for me instead of starting his own agency?" In other words, if he's got several years in the insurance industry as a talented, top producer, then it would only be logical to think that he should have his own book of business. If he has a substantial client base, then he should be making over $250,000 a year, minimum.

If he's an independent broker and he's making over a quarter of a million dollars a year, he won't be interviewing with you. So if he *is* independent, not working for another agency, then he's lying to you about his production and his level of past successes.

The only logical explanation for this is that he's been with another agency and is looking to leave and take his book of business with him. If he's with another agency, he'll probably tell you a sob story about how terrible his situation is and how he's been treated like a slave. He'll tell you that he's the one with the relationships with all the clients and that he could bring them over to you.

This is the gold-colored carrot he's going to dangle in front of you. But trust me, it's not a golden carrot. It's just gold-colored, and it's not even gold-plated.

It's fake gold paint on a rotten carrot.

I can't tell you how many interviewees have told me they've got this big book of business that they want to bring over to my firm. I can't even believe these guys are *that* stupid to tell me this.

If he's with another agency that has *any* sense at all, then they had him sign a producer agreement that has a noncompete/noncircumvention provision in place that would legally prevent him from taking clients with him.

So think about this. Right off the bat, he's telling you that he's going to attempt to screw his soon-to-be ex-employer. He'll tell you his employer is a jerk. He'll tell you he's not getting the support he needs from the agency owner. The reasons are irrelevant: he's going to intentionally break his contract and try to screw his boss.

Hello! If he's that kind of person and he's willing to screw his current employer, then it's only a matter of time before he decides he's going to screw you, too.

Don't be a sucker.

Don't let your greed overtake your integrity and better judgment. This is a wolf in sheep's clothing, and you'll regret dancing with this devil. That's one of the reasons why I don't hire people with insurance experience. They're coming in with a bunch of sob stories and a lot of baggage, and they'll expect you to be their bell hop.

Listen, if you want to be a professional baggage boy, then go get a part-time job working the curb at a luxury hotel. At least there you'll make tips.

I'm telling you: do not employ people with baggage.

Now, am I saying that you should never hire people that already have an insurance background? No, I'm not saying that at all.

If you find a guy or gal that is the right fit for your organization and they're coachable and hungry, fantastic. I've just found that most people with experience in the insurance world have preconceived ideas about how an agency should operate, and that preconceived idea is usually completely the opposite of the way I currently run my agency.

All of my producers (with the exception of one) were right out of college with no sales experience or insurance experience when they started with me. My *System-Driven Business* is responsible for ensuring their productivity and success. My producers weren't required to possess any knowledge, talent, or experience prior to coming to work for me.

People-Driven businesses tend to hold the business owner hostage, especially in an insurance agency. If your people start feeling like they don't need you or the agency infrastructure anymore, they'll eventually leave you. All of your hard work in developing and training them will have been in vain, not to mention both the hard and soft dollars you invested in them.

Your employees don't understand the true expense of running a business. I think it's important—especially for a business with less than fifty employees—to occasionally let the employees know how much things cost regarding business overhead.

Let me give you an example. My office is in an upscale, class-A, high-rise building. We pay over $14,000 a month in office rent.

When we first moved in, we were required to give the commercial landlord a $100,000 security deposit. This was a five-year lease, which meant that I had an $840,000 commitment in lease rents over these five years.

The Ethernet cables that we had installed for our internet service cost me over $8,000 just for the cables, not including the installation cost, which was another $3,500.

Running a successful business is expensive, especially in my marketplace (Orange County, California). In my opinion, it's important to let your people know this; otherwise, they won't appreciate what you do and what you're providing them regarding running and paying for the operation.

Why am I telling you this?

Because it all plays into the fact that you have to deliver value to your producers so they see that going out on their own isn't as easy as it seems on the surface. In the example I just gave you, I was illustrating the value (and expense) of running an operation, just from an infrastructure perspective.

But that's only part of it. You have to also deliver value to your producers from an access and content perspective. Let's talk about the difference.

Access

There is a lot of power in understanding and communicating the value of access.

What is access?

Access to carrier executives.

Access to underwriters.

Access to claims departments.

I have access to carrier information, industry information, and legislative information before it ever hits the streets. This access comes along with being a top producing agency with the carriers.

A one-man, independent broker/agent will never have the premium volume to warrant access to these types of resources that a larger agency owner is privy to. Access is powerful, and your people need to know that they have an edge by being associated with you because *you* have the access.

Many of my clients that I do business development consulting for boast their access to me in an effort to show their producers that they are part of a larger, more powerful entity. A lot of times, my clients that own insurance agencies weren't super agencies when they started working with me, so they didn't have the access I'm referring to.

So how do you recruit an army of producers when you don't have the credentials to back up your claim of being able to lead them to the promised land?

If you're a consulting client of mine, you can boast of your access to me. This is one of the most powerful things you can do when you're building your empire. You can use my credibility to enhance your credibility. In fact, I even recommend that my consulting clients give their producers a copy of a list of my client services, along with my rates. When their producers see the $50,000 price tag on the video-embedded PowerPoint presentation they've been using to close all that business or my $750 per hour consulting rate, they start appreciating what their boss (you) is doing for them—investing in them by paying my fees and giving them access to my training and consulting.

The second area that you should be boasting to your people is your ownership of great sales and marketing content.

Content

This dovetails in with what I just finished discussing regarding my consulting clients having access to me. In my own agency, I'm constantly developing new content for my producers.

What do I mean by content?

New sales scripts.

New sales and marketing videos.

New things that make their job easier and ultimately make them more money.

You see, my people know that I'm constantly evolving my agency to stay several steps ahead of the competition. This evolution of our overall operation and systems plays a huge role in our success as an agency, and my people know it.

This content is what I call Part of the System.

The entire system—what I call The *System-Driven Business*—is a top-to-bottom instructional process that governs every task that every person in my agency executes.

My producers know exactly what to say on the phone to book a sales appointment. They know exactly what to say when they're on that sales appointment.

They know exactly what to do in every scenario imaginable.

They know the chronology of what content is to be communicated and the style and medium in which that message is to be communicated, and they understand the philosophy behind why this method works.

They know *exactly* what to do and how to do it.

Now, think about your own business. When you hire a brand-new producer, on his or her first day of employment—the minute that producer walk into your office on his or her first day—do you have a specific step-by-step process to get that person started?

Think about your veteran producers. How well trained are they? Are they trained in a system that produces virtually the exact same result for every producer that goes through that training? Do your people have ultimate clarity regarding their jobs, their tasks, and what's expected of them?

Do they know *exactly* what to do? Do they know *exactly* how to do it?

On a sales call, do they know *exactly* what to say? Do they know *exactly* how to say it?

If the answer to any of these questions is no, then you don't have a *System-Driven Business*. You've got a People-Driven Business, which by definition, means that your people are being left to their own devices, and what usually happens when you leave people to their own devices?

They fail miserably. Now *you're* miserable.

Think about this: what percentage of the time do you find yourself frustrated with your business, your people, your clients, and your prospects?

I'm serious. Think through this question.

If you have producers, what percentage of the time do you find yourself frustrated that they're not producing enough, not working hard enough, or not committed enough? How much of your time is spent obsessing about how they just don't get it?

Think about your clients. How often do you find yourself frustrated that your clients are overdemanding, having a lack of appreciation for what you do for them? How often are you frustrated and stressed out because you have clients that are just a big pain in the butt?

How often is your day completely ruined because you had to spend a ton of your personal time putting out fires, fixing problems, and sucking up to your clients so they don't leave you?

Now think about your prospects.

How much time do you spend obsessing about prospects that are procrastinating, dilly-dallying, or frustrating the heck out of you?

How much time do you spend talking to your coworkers, friends, family, and worst of all, your spouse, about some stupid prospect that keeps putting you off?

Think about all of this time that you're spending obsessing about these things I just mentioned. Now think about what percentage of your overall business life is spent obsessing about these things. What percentage of your business life is spent being frustrated and stressed out about this stuff?

I've done business development seminars and sales coaching seminars all over the country, and the common response is 80 percent.

80 percent?

That means that 80 percent of your business life is spent in utter misery. This is no way to live.

When you first got into the insurance industry, I doubt you said to yourself, "Oh goody-goody. I can't wait to start spending 80 percent of the rest of my life in misery."

But that's where you are right now, right?

Don't feel bad. The majority of people in sales, regardless of the industry, are in the exact same emotional position you're in. They feel dejected, beat up, and burned out. I've been there myself.

But once I developed a better system—a systematic approach to not only my own personal sales, but also to the development of my agency—everything changed for the better. I went from virtually 0 to over $167,000 a month in renewal commissions within twenty-four months.

That's $167,000 per month, not per year.

The 3 Key Elements of a Great System

I realized from the very beginning that a great system could only truly be deserving of the adjective great if—and only if—it worked with virtually every single employee that followed that system.

In order to have that dramatic of an effect, the system would have to have the power to change the culture of an organization with little-to-no rebellion, which other people told me was virtually impossible.

Now, I'm not an idiot. I never said this was going to be easy. I just said I could do it, and I did do it.

That being said, there were several challenges along the way, but all of them were crushed by my determination, ingenuity, and understanding of human psychology, human behavioral patterns, and human thought processes.

Here are the challenges I had to overcome:

The first challenge revolved around ramp-up time.

Generally speaking, whenever you're attempting to either create a culture or a cultural shift, you need some ramp-up time to allow the new paradigm to trickle down into the organization, get accepted, get adopted, get implemented, and then ultimately get executed. The problem was that I didn't have time to allow for ramp-up time. I needed to go straight from design to execution.

The good news was that I have always done my best work under an insurmountable amount of pressure. As I thought through the design elements of creating a great system, there were three components that I found necessary to pull this off.

Component #1: A Great System Must Be Simple.

The first component to a great system is that it must be simple.

It must be simple enough to explain and simple enough to understand.

It must not contain too many moving parts.

It must be completely void of any element that isn't absolutely necessary.

It's got to be lean and mean. My systems are incredibly simple.

Now don't misinterpret what I'm saying. I didn't say they were simple and easy for me to develop. I said they were simple and easy to implement. That's the genius of a great system.

To illustrate this point, a friend of mine recently told me a story about Pablo Picasso. Apparently, Picasso was sitting in a café, doodling on a cocktail napkin. The waitress saw him sketching and asked him if she could have his sketch.

Picasso said, "Sure, you may have this sketch for $50,000."

The waitress replied, "$50,000! Are you nuts? That only took you a few minutes to sketch."

Picasso replied, "My dear, this sketch did not just take me a few minutes to sketch. This sketch took me a lifetime to sketch."

That's the value of what I call *simplistic brilliance.*

Now, I'm not likening myself to Picasso, but I will tell you that my business systems are simplistically brilliant.

It's the simplicity that allows for immediate implementation, immediate impact, and immediate results.

One of my larger clients is a $1.1-billion insurance company. I started doing business development consulting for them during the summer of 2009 on a variety of projects. My most recent project revolved around developing a new training program for their 6,000-plus agents across the country. In December, I finished developing some great new sales content to roll out at their annual kickoff meeting in January 2010.

It was December 2009, and I had just completed designing the new sales and marketing program for them. They wanted to run a test pilot using the program I developed for them prior to the January 2010 rollout. Now, December is just about the worst month you could possibly rollout a new program simply due to the holiday season, but they were adamant about wanting to test my program prior to the January rollout, so I went along with it.

They decided to do two days of pilot testing, which is not even close to the amount of time needed to test *most* new programs. It's just not enough time to (1) ramp up the program, and (2) gather enough statistical data to quantify anything substantial. In addition to these adverse conditions, they couldn't have picked two tougher days to test, and most new programs would fail under these circumstances. *My* program, though, wasn't *most new programs*.

The first day was Friday, December 18th, which was the Friday before the week of Christmas. The second day was Monday, December 21st, which was the week of Christmas.

Despite these adverse conditions, we ran the test anyway. I projected a 7–9 percent return during the first four to six weeks. In these first two days, my pilot tested at a 9.8 percent return. That's the beauty of a great system: virtually zero ramp-up time needed, immediate implementation, and immediate results.

Here we are in April 2010, and the first quarter numbers are in. After less than three months of my systems being implemented, their direct sales are up 53 percent over 2009's first quarter production.

Simplistic brilliance: Real impact. Real results.

Component #2: A Great System Is Specific.

The second component to a great system is that it must give people specific directives on what to do and how to do it. Think about my story at the beginning of this book regarding my frustration at trying to assemble my son's baby bouncer with poor instructions. I was confused and frustrated.

That's what happens to employees when they don't know *exactly* what to do or how to do it: they get frustrated.

People can only go on for so long being frustrated and confused before they quit. For most people, they'll last for two to four weeks before they quit. For others, they can't even last one day. Now, this is where I've made *huge* mistakes in the past.

I'd say to myself, "What a bunch of wusses." I'd get so upset that people couldn't stick it out, and I'd label them as weak. I'd say things like, "If they only knew how hard I had to work," or, "Nobody ever gave *me* a system on a silver platter, and I figured it out on my own." I'd even say things like, "People should be able to grind it out like I did."

Have you ever found yourself saying things like this?

If the answer is yes, then you've felt the frustration that I used to experience. This is the frustration of not having a *System-Driven Business*.

Yes, people should work harder.

Yes, people should be tougher.

Yes, people should be more creative and find ways to make things work.

The problem is that they *won't* work harder, they *aren't* tougher, and they will *never* be any of these things. You need to accept this, as frustrating as it may be. You need to accept this as the reality of life and design your business to accommodate this human deficiency. In fact, you should just erase the word *should* from your vocabulary because there are a lot of things people should do but will *never* do.

Should you have to spoon-feed them to this degree? Probably not.

Do you *have* to spoon-feed them to this degree? Not if you don't want to.

If you *do* spoon-feed them to this degree, will you build an army of producers that ultimately makes you wealthy? Absolutely.

In my organization, every word that comes out of my people's mouths is coached.

The content is coached.

The speech inflection is coached.

The speech rhythm is coached.

The voice volume is coached.

Everything is coached.

I teach my people why my method of communication works, what my philosophy behind each scripted word is, and how each script was engineered. I teach them the subconscious interpretation of each subtle linguistic pattern we use and why people respond they way they do.

You see, if you have a very specific method of communication, operation, and execution, and your people understand how to execute using your system, you've got a *System-Driven Business*. You've got a machine.

Your people will love you because they know that it is your system that is making them successful, and without you and your system, they'd make less money on their own. Now you're holding all the cards.

Your people will never experience the frustration of not knowing exactly what to do. They won't have that paralysis by analysis moment where they freeze up due to confusion and lack of clarity.

This is why it's so important to have a clearly defined SMO, or Standard Method of Operation. This is a taught method of how to prospect, close, and retain business. It is a trained set of rules that everyone in your organization must adhere to.

For example, in my organization, we never leave a proposal behind without a signed commitment from the client to do business with us. Never.

Why?

Because we know that at least 30 percent of the prospects we meet with are going to lie to us. They're going to lead us to believe that they're legitimately interested in doing business with us, when all along, they were planning to take our ideas back to their broker and cut us out of the deal.

I hate to admit it, but I do the same thing as a consumer. I'll spend an hour with a sales guy at retail store, asking him tons of questions about a TV, and then I'll go buy it online for a cheaper price. We all do this. That's why you never want to leave a proposal behind with a prospect unless they give you a commitment to do business with you by signing a contract. Don't allow them to waste your time.

This is just one example of several rules of engagement that I teach my producers to follow. This is part of our Standard Method Of Operation.

Your SMO must be very specific. Once everyone knows the rules, it's an easy process to execute because everyone knows exactly what to do, how to do it, and why we do it in this manner.

When I personally work with a client on a consulting basis, one of the first things I do is have them tell me what their SMO is. In other words, what is the process they go through from generating a prospect to procuring the sale to retaining the client. In most cases, they don't have a premeditated process. That's what they hire me for.

I create a simple, easy to follow method of operation so that all of their producers are marching to the same beat of the same drum.

When I create an SMO for my clients that I do consulting work for, I make sure that every person in their organization knows exactly what to do in every scenario imaginable. I've had so many of my clients tell me how amazed they were at how fast their producers adopted and implemented my systems and how quickly they were getting results.

In my opinion, a truly great system will yield you results within the first week, and sometimes, within the first day.

Component #3: A Great System Has Proof of Concept.

The third component of a great system is that it must have Proof of Concept. There's nothing I hate more than these wannabe, so-called sales trainers that teach things that they've never successfully done before. It makes me sick to my stomach.

Even worse, I've seen training programs that teach people to do things that haven't been statistically proven to work over time. When I question these people about the legitimacy of their training programs, they say stupid things like, "This should work."

My response is always, "If you're so confident, then test it for thirty to sixty days, and once you have the proof, then roll it out to everyone."

This usually infuriates them because they know I'm right.

I only teach things that have been statistically proven through vigorous testing and have produced quantifiable results.

That's why I just laugh at people that say, "Darren, I just don't think your system would work in *my* agency because of blah, blah, blah."

Okay, first of all, your opinion about my systems is meaningless.

Sound harsh? Bear with me on this one.

My *opinion* about what should or shouldn't work is also meaningless.

The only thing that matters is the truth—what has been proven to work. I don't base my teachings on opinions. I base them on proven, quantifiable statistics. I base them on the truth. That's it.

If the foundation of a teaching is merely based on someone's opinion, then it's complete garbage. On a recent project, a life insurance company contracted me to revamp, redesign, and rebrand their entire sales approach. They told me that they wanted me to change the culture of the company, which is a big undertaking, to say the least.

When I first designed my sales approach, I wrote a cold-calling script. I designed a video-embedded PowerPoint presentation to be used on a first appointment with a prospect. I designed this program to be completely dummy-proof.

The first push back I got was from the veterans in the company that told me that they just weren't a cold-calling culture. I guess they didn't get the memo that my job was to change the entire culture of the organization to a cold-calling culture.

They said, "Darren, it's obviously worked for you, but we sell *life* insurance. Your organization sells *health* insurance. It's different."

Yeah, whatever.

So we rolled this out in Newport Beach, California, at their territory office, and we got the exact results that I expected.

The next objection was that it was a Southern California thing and that it wouldn't work in the Midwest.

So we did it again in Chicago and actually got better results than we did in Newport Beach, California.

They balked, "Yeah Darren, but those are two big-city markets. This wouldn't work in a smaller, rural market."

So we did it again in Little Rock, Arkansas. Same results.

Tulsa, Oklahoma. Same results.

Charlotte, North Carolina. Same results.

Boston, Massachusetts. Same results.

Houston, Texas. Same results.

Dublin, Ohio. Same results.

Las Vegas, Nevada. Same results.

Have I made my point yet?

When you have a truly great system, it works wherever you go, in any market with any sales organization.

And just so you know, great systems contain concepts that work regardless of the industry because they're based on understanding human psychology, human behavioral patterns, and the human subconscious mind.

One of my clients, Kelly Smith (who is now a very dear friend of mine), is a brilliant corporate financial strategist in Newport Beach, California. I started working with Kelly about three years ago, revamping his sales and marketing approach. Last year, he was the number one producing Mass Mutual agent in the entire Western Region.

Another one of my clients is an educational software company. UEIS was founded by Dr. Sylvester Harris, a college professor who developed the first electronic standardized teacher evaluation program. This software application he developed is called TOR, an acronym for Teacher Observation Report. He and his team of professors have spent the last seven years developing this brilliant software application.

Their challenge, to their own admission, was that they didn't have a systematic way to build a national sales force, nor did they have a systematic way to market their product. They hired me to develop a recruiting program for them to attract sales reps all over the country. I developed a webcam interview process using Skype, teaching them how to properly conduct interviews for sales rep candidates. They had been doing conference call interviews prior to hiring me and had dismal results. When they first came to me, UEIS only had four sales reps. There's nothing more frustrating than having a great product but not having a big enough sales force to capitalize on the opportunity.

Sound familiar?

Anyway, they started using my recruiting system three weeks ago, and now they have fifty-eight sales reps in multiple states. I took them from four sales reps to fifty-eight sales reps in a period of less than four weeks.

I also developed online recruiting videos and a sales video for their sales reps to use to explain how the software application works. This powerful seven-minute video explains how the program works and includes brief interview clips with Dr. Harris and one of his clients that has been using his program. This video also includes a product demo, making it easy for a prospect to understand what the product does, how it works, and why it's superior compared to any other option.

The key to everything I'm talking about is systematizing every single process within your agency. When your people know exactly what to do and how to do it, you've got a *System-Driven Business*.

Sure, it takes some time to put all the pieces in place, and it doesn't happen overnight, but if you diligently build your agency using my system, one piece at a time, you'll end up with a super agency that is bigger, stronger, and more powerful than you ever dreamed of.

The ultimate goal, if you're an agency owner, is to build an agency filled with successful producers that can operate autonomously. You shouldn't have to baby sit your producers 24/7. You shouldn't have to touch every transaction that takes place in your agency.

If you have to touch every single deal that goes through your agency, then you don't have a business. You have a job. Sure, you're self-employed, but you're overworked, overly stressed out, and eventually, you're going to burn out. You're taking on the burdens of all of your people, and a single human being can't do that effectively, at least not long-term. You can't be everything to everyone 100 percent of the time.

Build the system, and the system will take care of the people, including you.

Chapter 4

Why Everyone Hates Scripts

Most people that I work with are initially very resistant to the idea of using sales scripts. I don't blame them; most scripts suck. I've read tons of sales scripts, and let me tell you, most of them are just awful. They sound fake, mechanical, and, well, scripted.

A great script is just the opposite. A great script sounds chit-chatty, feels slightly nonchalant, and always has an offer that is just too compelling to dismiss. A great script makes the prospect say, "Wow, that sounds pretty cool. Tell me more."

When creating a script, I'm hitting several subconscious triggers that make the prospect practically beg for the appointment. It's the engineering of the script that makes it brilliant and effective.

When I develop a sales script or an appointment-booking script for a client, I always walk them through each section of the script, explaining why it was engineered the way it was and what we're seeking to accomplish with each word.

Now, before I go into the fine art of script writing, let me say this: so many veterans in the insurance business (as well as veterans in other industries) will tell me, "I don't need a script. I've been doing this for twenty-five years, and I've never used a script." Gee, congratulations, buddy. You said you've been doing this for twenty-five years, right? I built a $37 million insurance agency in seven years. How much business have you done in twenty-five years?

Exactly.

It always baffles me when people want to argue with my methods. They know I have Proof of Concept, but they still want to argue with me. Even worse, sometimes I'll do a business development seminar, and someone in the crowd will always feel the need to come up to me after the seminar and tell me that they do exactly same thing that I just taught.

Yeah, right. *Exactly* the same thing?

I did $37 million last year. How much did you do? If you did *exactly* the same thing I've done, then you should have a $37 million agency too, right?

Okay, enough beating the dead horse.

It never ceases to amaze me that people's egos will get in the way of their own success. These people that say, "I don't need a script; I'm a pro," are basically implying that somehow, they're above using a script.

Hey, Tom Cruise uses a script, and the last time I checked, his 1099 was bigger than both of ours combined.

Movie stars read scripts everyday. That's what they do, and they make millions of dollars doing it. The ones that do a better job reading their script make several millions of dollars per film. Hey, if Tom Cruise isn't above using a script, then neither should you be.

There are two components of a successful script. The first is the content of the script. The second is the delivery of the script.

For example, have you ever seen the movie *Pride and Prejudice?*

Women love this movie. I've probably seen this movie with my wife over a dozen times. She absolutely *loves* this movie.

Women all say, "Mr. Darcy is so romantic."

Listen, honey, Mr. Darcy is a character played by an actor.

It's not him. He's not romantic. He's just reading a script.

Ladies, aren't you just crushed at hearing these words?

He's just reciting a script, but he's got you crying your eyeballs out.

Why? Because he's got a great script, and he's damn good at delivering it.

This combination—the script content and the delivery by the actor—has created strong emotions within you. That's what a great movie script does, and that's also what a great sales script does. They both create a specific emotion within you that you can't help but respond to.

Great actors have been known to do intensive research on their roles, learning how their character thinks, talks, and walks. They seek to really understand the mindset of their characters. Screenwriters are masters at creating scripts that tug at the human heart; they understand what people respond to.

That's essentially what I do. I understand what people respond to on an emotional level as well as on a subconscious level, and that's why my scripts produce immediate results.

What Makes a Great Script a *Great* Script?

There are several stages that a great script takes the prospect through.

The first stage is setting the emotional state. When you're cold-calling, the prospect is in a particular emotional state when they answer your phone call.

Do you think the prospect is in an emotional state of curiosity, intrigue, and excitement?

Of course not.

They're in an emotional state of annoyance, skepticism, and disinterest.

When you call a business owner or a decision maker on the phone, you have about a 95 percent chance that you're interrupting him right in the middle of a project. Business owners and decision makers are generally busy. They're not kicking back in their office watching Oprah and eating bonbons all day. They're working, and they're probably stressed out.

By definition, you're interrupting him.

Think about the emotional state this guy is in. Initially, it's not one of being ultra-receptive to hear about your great product or service … until we break him out of his current emotional state.

You have to break him out of his current emotional state in order to get him into the proper emotional state.

So how do you do this?

You do this by using the proper Emotional State Breaking Language (ESBL^{TM}).

One of the best emotional state breaking lines is, "I'm glad I got a hold of you." This creates positive expectation on a subconscious level. If I was to call you up in the middle of your day and say, "Oh, man! I'm glad I got a hold of you," your ears would perk up, and you'd be anticipating either good news or important news. Either way, your emotional state would be one of receptivity.

We use this same technique when cold-call prospecting. It makes the prospect subconsciously say, "Really! Why?" This doesn't happen at the conscious level, only at the subconscious level.

This is much better than starting the phone call off with, "Hi, this is John from XYZ corporation. How are you?"

Do you really think he thinks you actually care about how his day is going?

You're not fooling anyone. Plus, it comes off as disingenuous.

That's why I hate this suck-up approach. If it worked, I still wouldn't like it because I abhor the suck-up approach, but I'd have to say, "Okay, I guess sucking up works," but the truth is *it doesn't work.*

The key is to break them out of their emotional state and then hit them with a compelling offer that they can't say no to. They may not initially say yes, but they won't initially say no, either. The offer must be intriguing enough for them to not interrupt you or hang up the phone before you get your whole message out.

What this means is that you've got to spit out your message as fast as you can without them interrupting you. This process I'm about to explain to you is what I call BIT^{TM} Communication Technology.

BIT^{TM} Communication Technology:

BIT is an acronym for Benefit, Inside Story, Testimonial.

It starts with the offer, or the Benefit, as we call it.

The Benefit tells them what they're going to get out of the deal. Usually, the Benefit gives the prospect a financial incentive. For example, "Save money on your monthly bill." Typically, if you have a benefit that is really good for them, the most common objection is that it sounds too good to be true.

Since we already know this, our goal is to immediately tell them the Inside Story.

The Inside Story is the behind-the-scenes story that explains why the Benefit exists. It validates the legitimacy of the claimed benefit.

For example, the Inside Story behind our ability to save the client money could be a special program we developed, a new product offering, a change in legislature, or a change in the economy.

Inside Stories are most powerful when they revolve around something new: people love new. In marketing, the three most powerful words that command the strongest knee-jerk reactions are:

1. Free

2. Sex

3. New

Now, in the insurance world, you can't give away free insurance: it's illegal.

I highly recommend that you don't give away the second one: it's also illegal in some states.

So, we're left with the third one: new.

When the new body style of a car comes out, everyone wants the new body style. The old body style might be better than the new one, but it doesn't matter. People still want the new one.

Here's another example:

A few months ago, I purchased a video camera. Within a couple of weeks, it died on me, so I took it back to the store I bought it from. Fortunately, it was under warranty, so they told me they'd replace it with the same one.

The sales guy starts entering my information into the system to process the exchange, and then he says, "Well, your model has been discontinued, and we don't have any more of your models in stock."

I said, "Okay, I'll take the *new* model." I was actually pretty excited. I liked the idea of getting the *new* model.

The sales guy said, "The only problem is that we're not getting the *new* models until next week's shipment."

I said, "Well I've got a speaking engagement tomorrow, and I need a video camera right now."

So the sales guy told me, "Hold on a second. Let me do a search to see if another one of our stores has any in stock."

Then he says, "Ah-ha! The Costa Mesa store has two in stock. I'll call them right now and tell them to hold one for you."

I said, "Perfect! That's the *new* model, right?"

"No," he said, "it's the *old* one."

"The *old* one? Man, I don't want the *old*, discontinued, out-of-date, obsolete one. I want the *new* one."

Now think about this. I was perfectly happy with my video camera before it broke. It was great. All of a sudden, as soon as I learned that there was a *new* version, I *hated* my video camera.

I hadn't even seen the new one yet. Maybe the new one sucked. It didn't matter. I still wanted the new one. That's the way people are. Human beings are always intrigued by new things.

Most people want to at least find out what's new in the marketplace, just to find out if they're getting a good deal or a cruddy deal.

In my insurance agency, we're always talking to prospects about new products, new strategies, and new changes in the marketplace. Our entire message is constructed around the idea of giving business owners new opportunities to save money.

The other thing about the word new is that it implies relevance.

Current events and currently changing environments, by definition, mean that they are relevant today. People are generally resistant to change their minds and decisions about things, but they are actually very open to making new decisions based on new information. That's why we're always talking about new this and new that.

After we've created a buzz around the new product, idea, strategy, or program, we hit them with a Testimonial. This is basically a case study. You want to show them a real-life example of a client that got the exact same benefit that they want. This creates jealousy. It's this jealousy that creates Role Reversal.

You see, when the prospect realizes that you have something they want, and they don't know where else to go to get it, you have the power. They infer from our conversation that there is only one of us, and there are countless other prospects that desperately want what we have. When you do this effectively, the prospect will practically beg for the meeting. This is where the Role Reversal begins.

Role Reversal:

Prospecting in sales is just like dating. In the dating world, typically, women have all the power. Why? Because typically, the man is the one pursuing the woman. By definition, the woman has the power simply because she has the ability to reject the man's proposal.

By definition, the man is in the position of weakness because he is outwardly communicating that he wants the woman's phone number more than the woman wants to give it to him. The woman, at this point, is in control because she has walk-away power, and the man does not. He's practically begging for acceptance (and her phone number) because he's desperate.

Now, every woman will confirm what I'm about to say:

There is nothing more repulsive to a woman than a desperate man. I'm going to say that again.

There is *nothing* more repulsive to a woman than a *desperate* man. Desperation within a man makes a woman's skin crawl (in a bad way, not a good way).

In sales, you're in the exact same position as the desperate man, and let me tell you, there is nothing more repulsive to a prospect than a desperate sales rep. They can smell the desperation seeping out of your pores.

So what you need to do is reverse the roles. You need to be the one with the walk-away power. You need to be in the position of power. The question is, "How do I do this?"

It starts with creating what I call Positive Jealousy.

You need to communicate to the prospect that they might be getting a bad deal and that you're offering a better deal. That's the Benefit.

You then need to communicate that you have top-secret, behind-the-scenes information, not known to the general public and that this information is the reason why this Benefit exists. That's the Inside Story.

Then, you hit them with a real-life story of one of your clients that got that exact same benefit, and you reinforce to them that you're the only one that can deliver this product, service, or strategy. That's the Testimonial.

So, you've got them intrigued, curious, and jealous.

Once you create this Positive Jealousy, meaning that the prospect is envious of your client and the results you were able to produce for them, you have all the power. They want the Benefit more than you want them as a client. Jealousy is one of the most powerful human emotions. Use it in a positive way in sales and you'll triple the amount of business you generate.

Now they're jealous. Mission accomplished. All you have to do now is set the appointment.

As you probably already know, booking the appointment is not so easy unless you have a script with great sales language. That's where I come in. I create incredible scripts that generate guaranteed appointments.

The Appointment Booking Script:

The appointment booking script must have a strong close. You don't want to blow it here, or all of your efforts will have been in vain. Don't say something stupid like, "What I'd like to do is set up a meeting with you." First of all, no one cares what *you* would like to do. They only care about what *they* would like to do.

And don't say something suck-up like, "Would it be okay with you if I came out to meet with you?" This just screams desperation.

So don't tell them what you'd like to do. They don't care what you'd like to do.

Don't ask them to grant you permission either. You'll sound like a beggar. What you want to do is make suggestions.

Close with saying, "What probably makes the most sense is to get together and see if there's a fit," or, "Let's just see if there's a good fit; it'll only take about fifteen minutes." Suggestions are strong, but not overbearing.

Good suggestions just make good sense, and that's really what you're trying to accomplish with a prospect. You want them to say in their subconscious mind, "What the heck, I'll meet with you. What you said seems to make good sense, and if you can truly help me, then cool."

Lastly, you want to dictate the day and time of the appointment. Don't say something stupid like, "So what does your schedule look like?" This is just plain weak and desperate. It implies that you have nothing else going on and that you're available any day. It's like a guy asking a girl out this weekend, she says she's busy, and he says, "What about next weekend—or the weekend after that, or the weekend after that—because I've got *nothing* going on and I'm a desperate loser?"

What you want to say is, "Let me check my schedule here," and offer a date and time that works for you, not them. When you call a doctor's office to book an appointment, they don't ask you what your schedule looks like. They tell you when the doctor's next available opening is, and you eagerly jump at the opportunity and say, "I'll take it!" Why? Because you're afraid of losing the appointment slot.

That's what you want the prospect to do, and they should. They should jump at the chance to meet with you, assuming you have something of real value to give them.

You see, now the roles have been reversed. They're excited about meeting with you. They should be more excited about meeting with you than you are with them. Once you accomplish this, you're in a whole different league.

You used to be perceived as "the Desperate Guy in the Bar."

Now, you're Brad Pitt.

Everyone wants you, and you know it, and there's nothing they can do about it. You're in control. That's what a great script does: it puts you in control.

Chapter 5

Presenting vs. Creating an Experience

Presenting vs. Creating an Experience

I absolutely hate the term *sales presentation.*
Think about it.

Do you want to sit through a presentation? I don't either. It just sounds boring, and in most cases, sales presentations *are* boring. A presentation doesn't seek to connect or communicate. A presentation is just a bunch of fluff. Brochures, graphs, pie charts and all of that presentation stuff is meaningless if your message doesn't connect or resonate with the prospect.

Don't do sales presentations.

What you want to do is create an experience for the prospect—a unique, compelling experience that makes it clear to them that you are the only one with the solution to their problems.

How do you do this?

It all starts the minute you walk into their office to greet them, and most sales reps blow it right from the start. They thank the prospect for their time.

Never Thank the Prospect for Their Time

This is one of the biggest mistakes people in sales make. The first thing they do when they walk into an appointment is say, "Thank you for taking the time to meet with me today."

This is stupid.

This is illogical.

And this is what most amateurs do.

The reason this is not a proper greeting is because when you say, "Thank you for your time," it implies that the prospect somehow did you a favor by meeting with you.

The prospect did *not* do you a favor by meeting with you.

Let me ask you something.

If you end up doing the deal with the prospect, who's getting the better end of the deal? In other words, when you look at the value the prospect is about to receive by working with you, whether it be a dollar savings, a great service, convenience, etc., versus the amount of commission that you're going to personally make as the agent/broker, who's getting the better deal?

If you're getting a better deal than the prospect is getting regarding doing a transaction with you, meaning you're making more commission than the client is getting value, then you're a conman, and you should be kicked out of our industry.

The client should *always* get the better end of the deal.

If you're really looking to serve the client properly and ethically, the client should *always* get more value from doing business with you in comparison to what you're personally making in commissions. This being the case, the client should be thanking you, not the other way around.

You're the one that drove all the way out to meet with them. You're the one that put case studies together to show them creative ways to save money, enhance their benefits package, save money on taxes, etc.

By thanking them for their time, you're literally devaluing the service that you provide. You're establishing the wrong type of relationship dynamic from the very beginning when you thank them for their time.

When you meet with a doctor, does he thank you for taking the time to come into his office? Of course not.

The doctor is going to help you get healed. He's delivering the value of your good health. Sure, he makes money for doing his job, but you're the one that's getting the real value. It's the same thing with the service you provide to your clients.

If you just look at it in simple terms, whoever got the better end of the deal should thank the one that went above and beyond what would normally be expected. If you take me out to dinner, then I should thank you. If I took you out to dinner, then you should thank me. It's pretty simple.

It's so simple, but in sales, most sales reps don't even stop to consider the underlying message they're communicating when they thank a prospect or a client for their time.

Now, I'm not saying you should be rude. Not at all. What I'm suggesting is that you must change the language you use. Instead of saying, "Thank you for your time today," you should say, "I'm really glad we could get together today. I think we're going to be able to help you guys out."

It's just as friendly, and the best part is that when you say this, guess what the prospect will say in return?

They'll say, "Hey, thanks a lot for coming out here today." Now you can say, "You're very welcome." Brilliant.

Isn't it interesting how something so seemingly minor can make such a dramatic difference in the way you are perceived by the prospect? They will have a greater level of respect and appreciation for what you do, which is exactly what you want.

I know this concept of not thanking people for their time seems a bit counterintuitive, and it probably makes you feel a little uncomfortable because this is what you've become accustomed to doing for so long.

Listen, I'm of Japanese-American decent. Culturally, we thank the hell out of each other. If you think it's difficult for you to feel comfortable with this new line of thinking and communicating, trust me: it was a much harder pill for me to swallow due to my Japanese upbringing.

For example, in my culture, when you go to someone's home, you must bring a gift as a token of appreciation for being an invited guest.

Now, when they come and visit you at your home, they also have to bring you a gift as a token of appreciation for being your invited guest, but they will feel compelled to out-gift you. Their gift must be greater than the gift you gave them. Now you're screwed because if you get invited back to their home, you have to out-gift them. It becomes a vicious cycle of out-gifting the other, and before you know it, you're practically trading Ferraris.

Okay, that's an exaggeration, I admit. But the point is, we (Japanese people) are a culture that over-thanks each other.

I tell you this because it was very difficult for me to break away from this cultural norm in business. I admire and appreciate culture—remembering our past, and honoring our ancestors—but when culture stands in the way of progress, I have a problem with culture.

So as uncomfortable as this may make you initially, just change the phraseology you use, and watch how much your clients' perceived value of you and your services changes for the better.

Again, just tell them that you're excited about what you can do for them, and quite frankly, you should be passionate about what you do.

You should be excited about helping a client. That's your job. Just make sure you communicate that this excitement is based on the benefit that the client is going to get, not your commission check.

The Goal of the First Appointment

In the last chapter, I told you that the goal of a cold-call is to get the prospect to say, "What the heck, I'll meet with you. Let's see what you've got."

Well, okay. Now you're here.

You want the prospect to say, "Wow, this is cool. I've never seen anything like this before. If you can *really* deliver what you say you can, I'm in."

A sales presentation doesn't elicit this kind of emotion.

You have to create a unique experience for the prospect. Creating a unique experience involves surfacing certain emotions within the prospect. You're trying to create a new level of trust with the prospect.

Now think about this:

What advantage does the guy they're already working with have over you?

Familiarity. Familiarity breeds trust.

There's no way you're going to establish more credibility and trust with the prospect in a sixty-minute meeting than the other guy has established over several years, so don't try to build trust and rapport. You'll lose. Instead, get them to distrust their current broker.

How do you do this? Simply uncover the truth about the wrongdoings committed against the client by their current broker.

Uncovering the Truth

Here's an example of how to uncover the truth:

A guy meets a girl in a bar. The girl has a boyfriend. She's been with her boyfriend for five years. She's in love with her boyfriend.

There's no way the new guy is going to make this girl fall in love with him more than she already is with her current boyfriend, especially within a sixty-minute bar chat. There's no way she's going to trust this new guy over her boyfriend.

It takes a long time to build trust, would you agree?

But consider this:

How long does it take to destroy trust?

About thirty seconds.

If this new guy shows the girl digital pictures of her so-called boyfriend snuggled up in a dark corner of a restaurant with some hot blonde chick on a night where he was supposed to be hanging out with the boys, trust has been broken within a matter of seconds.

Why?

Because the new guy shined the light on the boyfriend's lack of character. Who's she going to trust more now: the busted boyfriend or the new guy who showed her the truth? She sure as heck doesn't trust the soon-to-be-ex-boyfriend anymore.

Now, she still doesn't completely trust the new guy either, obviously. However, the new guy is the only one left in the room, so by default, she'll trust him more than the soon-to-be-ex-boyfriend. By default, the new guy has established more trust—not complete trust— but more trust than the cheating soon-to-be ex-boyfriend.

That's the type of experience you want to create on a first appointment with a prospect. You want to uncover all the wrongdoings the incumbent broker has committed against the prospect. The prospect will now trust you more than the commission-hungry, lazy, incumbent broker. You just busted the incumbent broker.

I call this the Incumbent Broker Character Assassination.

The Incumbent Broker Character Assassination

Your goal should be to assassinate the character and integrity of their current broker, and in most cases, it isn't hard to do. Let's face it. Most brokers are complacent, lazy, and incompetent. All you need to do is uncover the areas where the broker has underperformed for the client. For example, ask the client why they think their broker didn't show them the new, creative ways to save money that you're showing them.

There are only two possible answers.

One, they didn't know these options existed, which means their broker is incompetent.

Two, the broker *did* know that these options existed, but they didn't want to lower the cost for the client because that would mean lowering their commission, which means their broker is money-hungry, greedy, and unethical.

So which one are they?

Incompetent or unethical?

Either way, the client realizes they've been taken advantage of, and they no longer trust their broker. If you're the one that exposed all of these wrongdoings, they'll trust you by default.

Bam! You just picked up a new client, and you haven't even asked for a census, run numbers, or delivered a quote or a proposal yet. You're winning over the client based on integrity, service, and performance, which is my entire brand.

You want to win over clients based on concepts and unique value-added services, not rates and benefits, and unlike most unscrupulous brokers out there, *not* taking advantage of the client's ignorance and naivety.

Let's talk very briefly about selling on price.

If you're trying to compete showing apples-to-apples comparisons, you're nothing more than a "me, too" broker. Anyone can generate a quote or a proposal. There's nothing special or compelling about that. You've got to show them something unique.

Now, that being said, you can show them a unique strategy that saves them money, where the emphasis is on the unique strategy. Sure, they may sign the deal over to you because the strategy saved them money, but this is different than selling on price alone. This is *not* apples-to-apples comparison selling. This is showing them a unique *strategy* that they've never seen before—again, emphasis on unique.

A lot of people get this confused. They'll see my selling strategy and say, "Darren, all of your producers sell on price."

To the amateur eye, I can see how they could misinterpret our process because the focus appeared to be on the cost savings. However, what the amateur eye is not seeing is that our selling process was actually *not* focused cost savings but rather the unique strategy that generated the cost savings. There is a big difference.

All of our so-called cost savings strategies are uniquely articulated and branded. They are all unique propositions that the prospect has never seen before, which is why they're signing the deal over to us, often times without even seeing a formal quote or proposal yet.

You see, you've got to have a Unique Selling Proposition (USP). A great USP answers the question, "Why should someone do business with you and only you? What can they get from you that they cannot get from anybody else?"

Once you answer this question, you have a USP. Now, you rule the world.

USPs are not cool, interesting, or different. They are unique. They are one-of-a-kind.

Once you establish the fact that the prospect wants what you have and they perceive that they can't get it from anyone else but you, you have accomplished the role reversal we talked about earlier.

The two easiest ways to establish trust with a prospect on a first meeting and create that unique experience we talked about earlier are:

Ask the prospect questions they don't know the answers to.

Show them things they've never seen before.

If you do these two simple things, you will have established yourself as the undisputed expert in the room. They will defer to you now because they realize that you know something that they don't.

You're the expert. Now you have the control.

Case Studies

Another key to creating an effective, compelling experience with a prospect on a first meeting is showing them case studies, examples of real clients you've worked with that have gotten real results using the exact same strategies that you're talking about.

Case studies are huge because they demonstrate Proof of Concept, which you know I'm a big fan of. Case studies are undeniable. Prospects can't look at a case study and say, "This isn't real." It *is* real, and it's staring at them right in the face.

The only objection they could have at this point is, "Yeah, but I just don't know if this would work for *our* company." That's a great reaction because all you have to say at that point is, "Well, let's find out and run the numbers using *your* company."

This proposition drives the next step.

Toward the end of the meeting—once you've dazzled them with all of these great ideas, strategies, programs, and case studies to back up your claims—they'll want you to run the numbers.

At this point, you want to book the follow-up meeting, which they should be begging for by now. Once you book the follow up meeting, you've given them something that you know they want—the chance to see if you can really help them or not. You can be assured that they believe in you now because if they didn't, they wouldn't have booked the second appointment with you.

Now you have what I call leverage.

What does that mean?

It means that you can take away that which you have given to them if they don't want to play the game by your rules.

You now have the power to dictate the next step.

If you require them to sign a Broker Exclusivity Letter or a Letter of Intent, you call the shots.

If you require them to sign a Master Application at this point, you call the shots.

If you have the guts to require that they sign a Broker of Record Letter at this point, you call the shots.

You see, when you have leverage, you call the shots, which means you're in control. You have walk-away power now because the prospect wants the opportunity to save money by working with you *more* than you want to work with them.

You are Brad Pitt, and everyone wants you.

Chapter 6

Consistency of Content

The 80/20 Rule

One of the things that every sales organization struggles with is the 80/20 rule.

Typically, 20 percent of your sales force produces 80 percent of your revenue, and the other 80 percent of your sales force contributes to you being frustrated 80 percent of the time in your business life. We talked about this earlier in this book.

So, what's the problem with the rest of your sales force? Why aren't they producing at the level that your big hitters are?

It's simple. They're just not as talented.

Your big hitters usually have a few qualities that the rest of your 80 percent don't have.

They have charisma. They're great with people. They tend to be good communicators. They tend to evoke feelings of trust and confidence within the prospect.

Now, the question is, "What exactly are they doing that the rest of your producers aren't doing?" Sure, they have these so-called qualities, but when you think about a first appointment with a prospect, how long does that appointment typically last?

It's usually about one hour.

Now think about this:

One hour is not that much time. So, if your top producers are producing drastically more business than the rest of your crew, the logical question would be, "What *exactly* are they doing in that first sixty minutes that the rest of your crew isn't doing?"

Another question you've logically got to ask yourself is,

"What are these top producers *not* doing in these sixty minutes that the rest of your crew *is* doing, and is the omission of this extra content the key to them being more successful? Is the omission of this extra, ineffective, verbose content the key to being more succinct and providing ultimate clarity leading the prospect to pull the trigger?"

If you could gather the exact content of every single successful sales appointment, if you could distill this content down to the most concise, tight, polished format, and if you could have every single producer duplicate that format, it would be like cloning your top producers over and over and over.

This is exactly what I've done. This is exactly why my agency shot from zero to $37 million in premiums in seven years, starting with absolutely nothing.

Think about this: I did it with a bunch of kids right out of college with no insurance experience, no sales experience, and very limited life experience.

Here's why I was able to do it and why you can, too:

Every word out of my people's mouths is coached.

The content of our message is always scripted.

Their communication style is a taught process.

Their speech inflection and voice tonality is coached and rehearsed.

This is what I call Consistency of Content, and the good news is that you can build your agency to the same level as mine by utilizing this powerful concept.

Consistency of Content

Consistency of Content, or C.O.C.™, is what makes my producers at my agency so successful. Every prospect gets the exact same experience during the prospecting process and the sales process, regardless of which one of my producers is interacting with him or her. Creating this unique, compelling experience is what we talked about earlier in this book.

There are several things that make our sales appointments so compelling, but perhaps the most compelling, the most unique, and the most effective component of our sales process has to do with the way we communicate, even more so than the actual content we communicate.

Now, don't get me wrong; our content is incredibly strong and compelling. Our USP is stronger than any company I've ever seen.

However, our communication process is even more compelling than the content itself.

Think about this:

How many times have you been told about a product where you had zero interest in the product, but then at a later date, someone that was actually using that product or service raved to you about how incredible it was?

They probably told you about all the problems they had with their previous product versus how great this new product was. They probably even *showed* you how it worked and pointed out all of the great attributes it had. After you experienced it, you had to have it.

Have you ever been through this type of experience?

I've experienced this countless times. I've had this experience when buying a TV. I've had this experience when thinking about buying a car. I've had this experience when buying a computer.

The amazing thing about this phenomenon is that in every one of these cases, the experience (the sales pitch) was never premeditated, rehearsed, or systematically executed. These experiences all happened randomly.

In business, I don't do *anything* randomly. Virtually everything is calculated, planned, rehearsed, and executed with precision.

One of the very few instances in marketing where a premeditated message is packaged and delivered in a systematic way so that every prospect gets the exact same experience every single time is in the TV infomercial world.

You may think TV infomercials are cheesy, and I would agree; most of them are.

However, do you have any idea how many Sham-Wow towels have been purchased through TV infomercials? What about Garden Weasels, ProActiv Skin Care products, and Juiceman Juicers?

In 1999, Billy Blanks and his workout DVD program Tae Bo did over $75 million in TV infomercial sales, and that was only in his first year.

In 2008, Bare Minerals (a TV infomercial cosmetic company) did over $400 million in the fourth quarter. That's over $400 million in sales within a three-month span.

What about Home Shopping Network? A good friend of mine got on Japan's HSN and sold over $200,000 worth of jewelry in twenty minutes.

Now, why are these numbers so astronomical? There are several reasons.

The Sham-Wow infomercial is the first that comes to mind. It's basically a guy doing a product demo, and he's actually kind of weird looking. In the infomercial, he's showing you how the product works. Essentially, here's the format of his message:

1. Here's what the product is

2. Here's what it does

3. Watch me use it

4. Watch me use it again

5. Here are some other ways you can use it

6. Here's the offer

7. Buy it now

Notice that he didn't spend time trying to build rapport with you. He didn't spend time talking to you about common interests. He just cuts to the chase, tells you what he's got, and if you want it, you'll buy it.

Not only is the content concise and straightforward, but the medium of communication through TV infomercials (and really any TV commercial) provides the prospect with Consistency of Content. Every viewer experiences the exact same content in the exact same medium with the exact same style of communication every single time.

Now, I know what you're thinking. No, I am *not* suggesting that you start running TV commercials to sell your insurance products.

My point is that the reason this communication medium is so effective is that it's an example of ultimate Consistency of Content, and in typical insurance sales, where producers (human beings) are the ones randomly shooting from the hip in sales appointments, there is no Consistency of Content whatsoever.

That's why I'm a big believer in using sales video content.

Sales Video Content

Earlier in this book, we talked about the power of video content. Yes, it is extremely powerful in the recruiting process online, but it is even more powerful in the sales process.

That's why I used the example of TV infomercials. Like them or not, they flat out sell. No doubt about it. They actually communicate the benefits of using the product they're selling, and they do it both effectively and systematically.

Often times, after they communicate the Benefit, they'll tell you the Inside Story of why the product works so well. Often times, they'll have people that have used the product telling their story about how the product has helped them, which is the Testimonial.

At the end of the infomercial, they'll have an offer, which is the close, and in this offer, they'll usually create some sort of urgency, like, "Call now in the next ten minutes and you'll receive an additional free widget."

Again, like them or hate them, TV infomercials do a lot of things extremely well from a sales and communication perspective. You can't argue with their sales success, but here's how this concept directly applies to my sales approach.

An infomercial is a concise message that statistically resonates with the target client. That's why I've converted the majority of our sales communication with the prospect into short, two- to three-minute videos.

When my producers go out and meet with a prospect face-to-face, they open their laptop and play a series of six short videos. Each video communicates a particular concept or strategy to the prospect. For example, one of our videos illustrates the mechanics of an Healthcare Savings Account (HSA) strategy. The video illustrates in a much more compelling format the same information that a producer would typically illustrate on a yellow pad and has a voiceover (my voice) explaining how an HSA works.

Here's why this is so effective:

The video is edited to perfection.

It's tight, concise, and very clear. It is the perfectly-engineered explanation of how an HSA works, so it's much easier for the prospect to understand this relatively complex concept.

That's one of the reasons HSAs have taken such a long time to catch on: simply because almost everyone I've ever heard try to explain how an HSA works has just butchered the explanation, including HSA administrators and their sales reps, not to mention brokers.

It's the inability to communicate concisely and clearly that has prolonged the adoption of HSAs, especially in the small business market.

The video I produced explaining the HSA concept is only one minute and forty-five seconds long. Trust me when I say this: no one could explain the mechanics of an HSA in less than ten minutes (let alone two minutes), and no one could communicate this concept more clearly than this perfectly-engineered and edited video.

The other great thing about using video communication in the sale process is that videos are always consistent in both their content and delivery. They are 100 percent perfect, 100 percent of the time. Using sales video content is the ultimate way to ensure C.O.C. within a sales organization.

Videos Provide Ultimate Consistency of Content

One of the challenges in professional sales is that you're relying on a human being to communicate concepts, and human beings are inconsistent.

Unless they are incredibly disciplined and scripted (which most are not), they're going to have a slightly different sales approach and format each time they step into a sales appointment, which means they have no Consistency of Content.

Not only do they lack Consistency of Content, but they also lack Consistency of Delivery.

Have you ever noticed that some days you're in the zone? You're just *on* that day, for whatever reason.

Have you noticed that some days, you're just off?

As human beings, we all have off days.

Why is that?

Because we're human beings, meaning we're susceptible to our emotions, and human beings are emotionally inconsistent. If you get into an argument with your spouse on the way out the door that morning, you're probably going to have an off day.

If you just lost a loved one, you're probably going to have an off day that day.

If you're recovering from the flu and you're feeling a little under the weather, you're probably going to have an off day that day.

Human beings have off days.

But videos never have off days. Videos don't get into arguments with their spouses. Videos don't have loved ones that pass away. Videos don't get the flu.

Videos are 100 percent perfect every single time.

The content is exactly perfect.

The tonality is exactly perfect.

The delivery is exactly perfect.

Videos don't babble and get off track. Videos don't lose their confidence. Videos don't forget what to say. Once edited, they are perfect.

Is this starting to make sense?

Videos Reduce Training Time

The other thing about video communication in the sales process is that it allows you to build an army of new producers that are game-ready almost instantaneously.

Essentially, all they have to do is show up on time and play the videos. The prospect is going to get the exact same experience—regardless of the producer's level of talent—simply because they're watching the exact same videos. That's one of the main advantages my producers have. It doesn't matter if it's me pushing play or a brand-new producer pushing play.

Sure, I'm more talented, more knowledgeable, and more confident than a brand-new producer, but it doesn't matter if the first appointment is structured so that the videos do the majority of the content articulation. My videos create the exact same client experience in the first meeting regardless of which producer is running the meeting.

The video is the one delivering the sales pitch, not the producer.

Videos Develop a Better Relationship Dynamic

As I just said, the video is the one delivering the sales pitch, not the producer. In my sales process, after each three-minute video is played, my producers chat with the prospect about the content they just viewed together.

This chatty conversation is much less combative than when a producer is trying to close the prospect in a typical sales scenario. When a producer is trying to close the prospect, it's kind of a cat-and-mouse game, almost as if the producer was in opposition to the prospect. No wonder the prospect resists.

When the prospect watches a video with the producer, sitting side-by-side (as opposed to sitting across the conference room table in opposition), the prospect feels like the producer is on their side.

Each video generates a low-key, comfortable, chatty conversation. The prospect wants to talk about what they just saw in the video versus a typical sales appointment where the producer desperately tries to win over the prospect by attempting to talk him or her into the deal.

The harder the producer tries to convince the prospect, the more desperate the producer appears. As I always say, in the dating world, there is nothing more repulsive to a woman than a desperate man. In the sales world, there is nothing more repulsive to a prospect than a desperate sales rep.

So right off the bat, the videos completely change the dynamic of the conversation in the sales appointment. There are several other subconscious triggers that videos pull in the sales process. Let's discuss a few.

Human Beings Are Obsessed with Video Monitors

I don't know why this is, but it is an undisputed fact that people are obsessed with looking at video monitors. If there is a TV screen, regardless of what's playing on it, people are drawn to look at it. They can't help themselves.

As I mentioned earlier in this book, when you're on an airplane and the flight attendant does the seat belt demonstration right before take off, nobody pays attention. But when that exact same demonstration is playing on a video screen, more than half of the people stare at the monitor, watching the video. These are the same people that would totally ignore the flight attendant standing in the aisle doing a live demo.

Recently, a friend of mine told me that he was at church one Sunday morning. He goes to one of those megachurches you see on TV with tens of thousands of attendees in the audience.

There were two big projection screens on stage with a live video feed of the pastor playing on them. Well, apparently the pastor was delivering his message and he started poking fun at the people sitting in the front row because there he was, standing right in front of them, live and in person, but none of the front row attendees were looking at him as he spoke; they all looked right past him, watching him on the huge projection screen directly behind him on the stage.

The pastor jokingly said to them, "Hello! Guys, I'm right here in front of you. Why are you looking at the video feed of me on the screen when I'm right here?" This story illustrates my point about our obsession with video monitors and video screens. We just can't stop looking at them.

That's why sales videos are so powerful. As illogical as it sounds, we've found that our prospects are more engaged with the content in the video (played on a laptop computer) than they are when a live human being delivers the exact same content.

I know this is somewhat counterintuitive, because you would think that people would have a greater connection with another human being versus a video screen. Ironically, they do not.

My Initial Concern with Using Videos

Initially, when I started testing this process, my concern was that business owners might view this process as being cold and impersonal. I feared that they would get bored sitting through so many videos. The reaction we got from our prospects was just the opposite. They absolutely loved it.

I think the reason they loved it is that my videos are so well done. I know this sounds like I'm patting myself on the back pretty hard (which I have been known to do quite often), but my style of video production is very distinct and quite brilliant.

I have a formula for engineering and producing these videos—everything from the storyboard of the video concept, to the type of background music playing, to the scripts I write for the voiceover—all the way down to how many seconds each screenshot plays before it cuts to the next screen shot.

This is part of what I do for my clients that hire me to do business development consulting for them. I produce incredible sales video content for them, and the results that my clients get from this content and this process are incredible. It enables them to not only increase their closing percentage in the field, but it also allows them to recruit and train new producers much more effectively and efficiently.

It allows them to control what is being communicated to their prospects as well as how it is being communicated. It gives them the ability to clone top producers because the video content is what is closing the business, not the personalities of their producers.

I know this is difficult to imagine without actually seeing these videos yourself. If you have the opportunity to ever attend one of my workshops or one of my Boot Camp Sales Training Events, you will see firsthand what I'm talking about, and it will blow your mind. You can also see some examples of my work on my website at www.DarrenSugiyama.com.

When I first started testing this process in my own agency, I was a little nervous because I had no idea if this would work or not. However, when we looked at our results within the first four months of getting this process dialed in, all doubt was removed.

In this four-month run, one of my producers closed a total of thirty-seven Broker of Record Letters without even running quotes. This is just one producer's results over a four-month period. Another one of my producers closed forty-two new accounts within this four-month period. These BORs were taken over simply by playing my series of sales videos. Why did they get such great results?

The reason is that the videos articulated the main reasons why a prospect should become a client of my firm. This is an example of how powerful video communication can be in streamlining, systematizing, and controlling the sales process.

Chapter 7

Building a Culture of Success

How Important Is Developing a Company Culture?

One of the most important elements in building a successful insurance agency—or well any company in any industry, for that matter—is establishing a distinct company culture.

What exactly is a distinct company culture?

It's the way people think.

It's the way they talk.

It's the way they walk.

It's their value system.

It's the way they view the world.

It's the way they dress.

It's the company's image and brand.

When I first started my firm, I spent the majority of my time obsessing about developing the right company culture. This focus was the driving force behind virtually every decision I made, both in my business life and in my personal life. Every decision, no matter how seemingly insignificant, was made by asking myself the question, "How does this affect our culture, and is it synonymous with my brand?"

I'm talking about *every* decision.

When I picked out our conference room chairs, I thought about who would be sitting in them and what image I was trying to project about my brand.

When I bought my car, I thought about what statement I was making and whether or not it was synonymous with my brand.

When I chose the music playlist on the sound system in our office, I thought about what mood I was trying to set and whether or not it was synonymous with my brand.

Let's talk about my brand for a moment, just to give you an idea of how important I believe this element is in your business.

When I think about office décor, I think about who my target client is who I'm trying to make an impression on. In my business, our actual clients (the insured employer groups) rarely ever come into our office, so my target clients, as it relates to office environment, are not our employer group clients.

My target clients are:

1. My interviewees

2. Carrier executives

3. Joint venture partners

4. My employees

Of these target groups, the most important group for me to market to is my own employees. When I think about my employees, I have a very distinct culture that I focus on perpetuating.

We work hard and fast, but we're not hustlers.

We talk loud and fast, but we're not fast-talkers.

We're focused on being financially successful, but we're not money-hungry.

We're very professional, but we're not corporate stiffs.

We're polished, but we're not plastic.

We enjoy luxury, but we're also in the trenches, grinding it out.

When we picked our office space, I wanted my employees to walk in the front door and feel like big shots. I wanted them to feel powerful and successful. So, we chose a class-A, high-rise building with an amazing panoramic view of Orange County, right by the airport.

I felt this was important because I wanted my employees—specifically my producers—to feel confident and successful. I wanted my people to work in an environment where they were surrounded by luxury.

Is it expensive?

Of course it's expensive. But you have to look at these types of business expenses and ask yourself whether you're going to get a good Return On Investment or not. In this particular area, as well as other areas that I'll discuss in this chapter, the answer is *absolutely*.

The Car You Drive

When I buy a car, I always take into consideration my target audience, and in this case, as the leader of an organization that is sales-based and 100 percent commission-based, my target audience is my sales producers.

Sales producers need to see a lifestyle that motivates them to want more. That's the main reason my top producers and I all drive luxury cars that cost $100,000 and up. It reinforces our brand, and as top producers and leaders of my organization, they understand the effect this has on the growth of our agency.

When a new producer interviews with you and you have a 100 percent commission-based opportunity, the only reason they're going to even consider this type of position that doesn't give them a base salary is that they have a dream of making more money than a regular cubicle job. That's why they're willing to work on straight commission.

So what they're telling you right off the bat is that they want the finer things in life and they're willing to take on some risk for a greater reward. They're willing to sacrifice in the beginning because they want the great life. Like it or not, they're going to size you up (as well as your top producers) and judge your opportunity based on the material trappings of success that they see. They're going to judge your tree based on the fruit. That's why you've got to show them some big shiny apples.

You can't blame them. It's only logical.

You're trying to sell them on the dream of being extremely successful, but if you don't have the external trappings of success, they're going to question your opportunity's financial potential.

You may say that only a superficial person would do this, but let's be honest: that's how people size each other up in business.

You're not going to show them your bank statements or your retirement fund, so you've got to show them something that they're going to see every day—something that they want—and most people like the idea of driving a luxury car. It's what they fantasize about. It's a status symbol.

You may say that it's not financially prudent to spend $1,800 a month on a car payment (which is what the lease payment is on a $100,000 car), and if you weren't trying to inspire sales producers to sell millions of dollars of insurance (or any product for that matter), I would agree with you. It is absolutely stupid to spend that much money on a car to impress your friends. But in business, you have to look at the Return On Investment.

The car payment on a Honda Accord is about $300 a month, so you'd be spending $1,500 more per month to drive a $100,000 luxury car. That's $18,000 a year in additional expenses (most of it tax deductible, by the way).

But what if you just attract *one* more producer to work for you?

If just *one* more interviewee sees that hot car and he or she buys into the earning potential that comes with working for you because he or she see you driving a hot car, how much more revenue would one good producer generate?

It should be a hundreds of thousands of dollars per year.

So in this case, spending $1,500 more per month on your car was a wise business investment because it gave you a huge Return On Investment. How much did the car really cost you?

Not only was it free, but it actually made you a handsome profit. Again, a car, if used properly, can be an effective business tool. It's a recruiting tool.

You wouldn't cheap-out on a tool that increases your business revenue, so don't cheap-out on your car. It's a statement that says, "My decision to be in this business allowed me to be able to afford this luxury car, and if you work hard, you could have a sweet car like this, too."

If you drive a cruddy, nondescript car, the message you're sending your producers is, "I know I told you that you can make a lot of money in this business, but I've been doing this for ten years now, and I can only afford to drive an economy car."

Whether that's true or not, that's their perception, and when it comes to recruiting new producers and inspiring current producers, that's the message you're sending when you're not driving a luxury car.

It's the same thing with a nice office. People walk in—specifically interviewees—and they're going to size up your operation based on how your office looks. Remember: these people just came from interviews with Northwestern Mutual, New York Life, and Bank of America. These are big name companies with credibility. Their opportunity might not be as good as yours, but that's not the point. It's what the interviewees perceive unless you do something about it.

In the beginning, maybe you don't have the money to invest in a high-rise, class-A office building. That's okay. Just do what I did.

I had a nice BMW, and I met with people in the lobby of a luxury hotel in Newport Beach.

The recruits saw what I was driving: a BMW.

They experienced a luxurious meeting environment: a luxury hotel.

They saw someone who looked successful: me in a suit and tie. In business, people only see:

1. What you're driving
2. Where you're meeting
3. What you're wearing

Don't sacrifice any of these three areas *ever*. If you don't have a nice office yet, pick somewhere to meet that's free and luxurious. Meeting in the lobby of a nice hotel isn't any more expensive that meeting someone at a cheap restaurant. In fact, it's cheaper because your interviewee won't order any food and stick you with the bill.

And when it comes to dressing for success, you've got to be an absolute moron to think that you look successful when you're not in a suit and tie, especially in a business environment. In fact, let's talk about dress for a moment.

The Power of Dressing for Success

My goal is to always be the best-dressed person in the room. Why? Because people respond to perceived power, and the way you dress is one of the most influential components of perceived power.

I get a lot of criticism when it comes to this topic, especially in Southern California, where business-casual is the norm. Some people say that you don't need to wear suits and ties in a business environment anymore. Hey, I agree. You don't have to wear a suit and tie. You can get away with business-casual.

But explain this to me:

I was sitting in a seminar with about one hundred people a few months ago in Newport Beach, California. I was not a speaker at this particular seminar; I was merely an attendee. It was on a Saturday afternoon, and the majority of the attendees were dressed in business-casual attire. The only people at this seminar that were wearing a suit and tie were the speaker, the owner of the company hosting the seminar (who is literally a billionaire), and me.

A couple of interesting things happened during this seminar. The owner of the company (the billionaire) came into the hotel banquet room where the seminar was hosted, looked around the room, and who did he decide to sit next to? Me.

He had no idea who I was, but he chose to sit next to the only other guy in the seminar who was wearing a suit and tie. Gee, I wonder why.

During the lunch break, I went through the buffet line and sat down at a semi-occupied table. The speaker then entered the room, went through the buffet line, and who did he decide to sit next to? Me.

It is an undisputable fact that successful people trust people that are dressed in formal business attire more than those dressed in business-casual attire. When you're dressed to the nines, successful people give you a higher level of respect. In sales, who are you meeting with primarily? Business owners who by definition are successful.

One of the stupidest things I've heard people say is that you want to dress like your clients and that if you're meeting with a blue-collar manufacturer that you shouldn't go in wearing a suit and tie. That is just plain stupid.

Think about these celebrity gangster rappers. Do you think they want their attorney dressed in baggy jeans, wearing a bandana around his head with a giant diamond encrusted medallion dangling from his neck? Of course not.

They want their attorney to be dressed like an attorney, not a gangster rapper. Even your blue-collar widget-making clients subconsciously want you to dress the part of a financial/insurance professional, not a widget maker.

I've had clients tell me not to come back to their office wearing a suit and tie.

So, what do I do?

I show up in a suit and tie anyway. That's who I am. Besides, they respond better to me when I look like a financial guru. If I was interviewing to be a blue-collar widget maker, that would be a different story, but I am not. I'm the financial guru, therefore I dress the part. You're always going to be better off in a suit and tie. Argue with me if you want, but you'll be wrong.

Casual Fridays

Casual Fridays could be the dumbest thing ever thought up.

First of all, Casual Fridays does not work.

Studies have shown a significant decrease in employee production when Casual Fridays is implemented. People will argue with me on this, saying that when people feel more comfortable, they're more productive. That's just stupid, unsubstantiated, ignorant rhetoric, but for the sake of this illustration, let's just say they're right and I'm wrong.

If that's truly the case, why don't we just make *every* day casual day?

If people really do perform better when dressed casually, then why are we dressing in suits and ties Monday through Thursday? Under this assumption, it would mean that we're intentionally sacrificing 80 percent of the production week (four of the five workdays) by wearing clothes that make us less productive and less comfortable.

Do you see how stupid this is?

Even those people who say Casual Fridays is a good idea quickly realize the illogic of their previous opinion when I propose that every day be casual.

Still not convinced?

Okay, let me show you an example of why dressing for business gives you an advantage. Virtually every time I walk into a meeting on a Friday and I'm dressed for business and the person I'm meeting with is dressed casually, guess what the first thing they say is when I shake their hand.

They usually say, "Oh, I apologize for the way I'm dressed. You know, it's Casual Friday here."

I always say, "No problem."

Think about how this meeting is starting out. They're apologizing to me, which instantaneously gives me the power.

Whether you like it or not, every meeting is based on a power struggle. One party is trying to get the other party to do something. There's always some sort of offer, negotiation, or settlement taking place. Wouldn't it make more sense to give yourself every edge you possibly could?

Now if you don't take your business all that seriously and you don't care about maximizing your results, then go ahead and dress in business-casual attire.

Go ahead, throw on your golf shirt (or even worse, your Hawaiian shirt) and your khakis. While you'll look like you're going to a luau, I'll look like a *real* businessman.

A guy like me who's wearing a custom-tailored navy blue suit will walk into your client's office and sixty minutes later walk out with a Broker of Record Letter and eventually take over all of your clients.

Dressing For Business Is a Formula-Driven Strategy

People often ask me if I have a formula for dressing for success in the same way that I do for virtually every other element of my business. Of course I do.

For men, the navy blue suit, white shirt, and red tie combination evokes greater balance of power and trust than any other combination. This is not my opinion or my personal fashion statement. This is a statistically proven fact.

Don't believe me?

Look at every televised presidential debate. Look at what the candidates are wearing. Navy blue suit, white shirt, and a red tie. Do you really think this is a mere coincidence?

Psychological studies have shown that this combination has statistically worked better than any other combination for this specific purpose. In this scenario, what these presidential candidates are attempting to accomplish is very similar to what you're trying to accomplish in a sales appointment. They're trying to gain power and trust. I teach my producers to stick to this formula-driven business attire.

Think about this:

Have you ever seen a guy wearing a suit and tie but he just looked frumpy and low-level? He probably wasn't wearing this combination of the navy blue suit, white shirt, and red tie.

If you really want to take this to the extreme, look at airline pilots. They generally wear a blue suit, a white shirt, and a solid-colored tie.

Now, when you really think about it, why are airline pilots so highly respected?

If you look at their role, they provide a service similar to that of taxi cab drivers, limousine drivers, and bus drivers. They just do it in the sky. Why are they so highly respected?

Same thing with flight attendants. What exactly is the difference between what a flight attendant does and what a cocktail waitress does, other than the fact a flight attendant does it on an airplane?

Now, if you're a cocktail waitress, or a flight attendant, or an airline pilot, don't be offended by what I'm saying.

This is purely a sociological observation comparing societal respect levels of different career types, not a personal judgment on you. All I'm saying is that when you see a pilot dressed in a navy blue suit or a flight attendant in a navy blue skirt suit, subconsciously, you respect them more than bus drivers and cocktail waitresses.

This is not an accident. This is an intentional, premeditated wardrobe strategy that the airline companies are using, and they're using it in the same way presidential candidates strategically wear navy blue suits.

Now, every once in a while, people will see me wearing something other than a navy blue suit, white shirt, and red tie, and they'll often ask me why I'm not practicing what I'm preaching.

I will often wear another combination when I'm not selling in a one-on-one environment, whereas my sales producers are in a one-on-one selling environment over 90 percent of the time. When you're in sales, the majority of your prospect interaction is going to be one-on-one, face-to-face with strangers that are meeting you for the first time, thus I recommend the blue suit-white shirt-red tie combination.

Another reason I recommend this is that many people starting out their careers can't afford to have my tailor make them $3,000 custom suits and $275 custom shirts. They're not going to drop $250 on a tie.

That being the case, you can get an inexpensive navy blue suit for around $100–$200, have it tailored for another $50, and look pretty damn good. You can get a simple white dress shirt for about $40 and a basic red tie for about $20. If you go this route, it's unlikely that you'll screw it up.

However, if you try to look more fashionable and you're wearing a $200 non-navy blue suit, you're probably going to look like you're wearing a cheap suit.

If you're wearing a cheap tie with a pattern on it or a cheap shirt in a funky color (like salmon or olive green), you're going to look like a guy in a cheap suit and tie.

For example, I love the look of a classic, beautiful, solid navy blue suit, a crisp white shirt with a spread collar and French cuffs, and a textured navy blue tie. If you do this right, this can be a very elegant look, but if you do it wrong, you'll look like a limousine driver or a security guard.

That's why I say that in the beginning stages of your career, before you're ready to drop $3,000 on custom suits and $250 on ties, stick to the navy blue suit, white shirt, and red tie. You can't go wrong.

The Dialed-In Wardrobe

Okay, so I addressed the guy just starting his career that doesn't have a lot of money yet. But maybe you're a guy that *can* afford to build a beautiful wardrobe and you're at the level where you want to *really* look the part.

I can't tell you how many people comment on my business attire. I probably get four to five compliments per week, which doesn't even include the nonvocalized admiration. In addition, my wardrobe has a subconscious effect on people that with whom I meet, and understanding that subconscious effect is the basis of my business wardrobe strategy.

Yes, that's right. I have developed a business wardrobe strategy. Sounds a bit over the top, right? I assure you that it is not over the top, and I can also assure you that the results I get using this strategy *are* over the top.

Why am I so adamant about the way I dress?

Because it's a reflection on me as a businessman, it's a reflection on the level at which I do business, and it is part of my personal brand. Most people don't place as much emphasis on the way they dress as I do, which is a huge mistake.

Let's discuss my business wardrobe strategy.

Think about golfing. You wouldn't tee off with a sand wedge. You wouldn't use a driver to get out of the rough. You wouldn't putt with a nine iron.

You use a very specific club for a very specific application in a very specific scenario. Each club is designed to accomplish a specific goal when you find yourself in a specific situation. That's the way I look at my business attire.

In my business, I play several different roles, and I find myself in several different scenarios with people. I adjust my business attire accordingly.

The *Showtime Suit*

Often times, I'll be the keynote speaker at an event. I may be speaking to several hundred people at a time from a stage.

In these cases, approximately 70 percent of the people in the audience have never met me before. In this scenario, my number one goal is to be perceived as the most powerful person in the room.

The spotlights are on me, the cameras are rolling, and it's showtime. There might be some people in the room that are skeptical about what I'm teaching from stage, so my goal here is to pull rank on them. Right off the bat, I have to build credibility in one area and one area only, and that area is Level 10 Success. The way I dress must overtly say, "I'm the most powerful person in the room, and I'm going to let everyone know it before I even open my mouth."

In this scenario, where establishing power and authority is the main objective, a bold-striped navy blue suit is best. It's loud, but from stage in front of a large group, it's a very strong and bold statement. I call these bold-striped suits *Showtime Suits.*

Showtime Suits should always be accompanied with a bright red or gold tie. If you're strong and you have exquisite taste, a pink tie works well here, too, but it has to be the right pink tie or you'll just look silly.

With a *Showtime Suit*, you should always wear either a white shirt or a colored shirt with a white collar. The white collar reads well from stage. I know a lot of guys like to wear nonwhite shirts because they think white shirts are boring. Again, if you have exquisite taste and you're going to spend $250 or more on a shirt, you might be able to get away with a nonwhite shirt, but if you don't do it with a white collar, you're a fool. A nonwhite collar just doesn't convey the power and wealth that a white collar does.

So again, if your main goal is to establish power, do it with a bold-striped suit, a white-collared shirt, and a bright tie.

The *Power Player Suit*

Sometimes I'm meeting a small group of four to five people for the very first time, either in a restaurant or in a small conference room.

In this scenario, my goal is to establish power, similar to speaking from stage to a large group. I want them to perceive that I am very good at what I do; however, in a small group environment, a bold-striped *Showtime Suit* can be too overpowering, especially on a first meeting.

In this scenario, a chalk-striped navy blue suit is more appropriate. This is a pinstriped suit, but the pinstripe is fainter. It still says, "I'm the most powerful person in the room," but in a slightly more subtle tone. I call this type of suit a *Power Player Suit.*

The chalk-striped navy blue suit establishes you as the person that should be sitting at the head of the conference room table. It says to everyone, "I'm running this meeting. This is *my* meeting."

This can be done with the same shirt and tie rules I laid out with the *Showtime Suit*. Now, if you're meeting with people that are also dressed to the nines, the *Showtime Suit* with the bold stripe works just fine, even in a small setting, if—and only if—your own personal brand is strong and aggressive.

I typically wear *Showtime Suits* whenever I'm in an important meeting with more than one person, even if it's a small venue. My personal brand is very strong and tends to be centered around the idea that "too much is never enough," and thus *Showtime Suits* are synonymous with my brand.

If you like the idea of being that strong and your audience is not typically a product buyer that you're meeting with for the first time, then perhaps *Showtime Suits* should be your *Everyday Suits* as well. If you're in a high-powered negotiation scenario and your target audience is sizing you up in terms of perceived power, then rock the *Showtime Suit* all day long.

However, if your target audience is a prospective buyer (i.e., an insurance prospect), *Showtime Suits* do not reflect the image you want to convey. Go with a solid navy blue suit, which is what I call the *One-On-One Suit.*

The *One-On-One Suit*

For people in face-to-face sales, the best (and most versatile) suit is a solid navy blue suit. I call this the *One-On-One Suit.* This is a classic look and translates competency and expertise.

In a one-on-one scenario, which is what most sales prospecting meetings are, the goal is to establish a combination of trust in both your integrity and your competency. In this intimate setting, you want your prospect's focus to be on your message, not your fashion sense. The message you're trying to convey is, "I'm the expert. Period."

Your goal is to get them to do business with you, which is based on your skill, professionalism, and trustworthiness. Sure, power is an element of your skill, but you're not trying to pull rank on your prospect. You're trying to get them to do exclusive business with you, which is done by establishing the perfect balance between trust in your integrity and trust in your competency.

When you walk out the door, you don't want them to remember what you were wearing. You just want them to remember that you are the expert with whom they should be doing business. Again, the focus should be on your ability, not your fashion sense. The focus should be on your message, not you.

Unlike the *Showtime Suit* and the *Power Player Suit* with which the focus is on branding yourself as a power player, the *One-On-One Suit's* focus is on the product or service that you're selling. Don't let your ego get in the way on this one.

In sales, you're more powerful if the focus is on the product or service you're selling than if the focus is on you.

If you're doing a joint venture, merger, or acquisition, and your goal is to send the message that you have the power to set the terms of the deal, the focus is on you, in which case you should wear the *Showtime Suit* or the *Power Player Suit.*

With the *Power Player Suit* and the *One-On-One Suit,* the white-collared shirt is important. The red tie is essential unless you have the right blue tie. There are a lot of wrong blue ties out there, so my general advice is to stick to the red tie.

Trust-Building Suits

Lastly, you may find yourself in a scenario where you're meeting with people with whom you're already doing business. You don't need to pull rank on them, and you don't need to build any more credibility with them.

But in some circumstances, you want to establish more trust with them. You want them to feel comfortable with continuing to do business with you without diminishing your professionalism. In these scenarios, a grey suit works extremely well. It says, "You already know that I'm powerful. I want you to know that I'm also approachable."

This is a great message to send if you're having a business dinner after a conference or if you're meeting with people of significantly lower rank within your company. For example, in the insurance business, you may be meeting with the employees of a company to do an enrollment. This would be a good time to wear a *Trust-Building Suit.*

Again, this suit is professional and commands respect in a nonthreatening way. It doesn't say, "I'm Mr. Power Player." It subtly says, "You can trust me."

A white shirt works best in this scenario, with a maroon or burnt orange tie.

Understanding your audience and understanding how you want to be perceived by this audience is imperative when strategically maximizing a positive response. Your business wardrobe sends a message, so you want to make sure you're sending the *right* message.

Your Audience

There are four categories of people you dress for. The first one is obvious. It's sales prospects.

You want your prospects to perceive your visual presentation as congruent with your company image. This is part of your brand, and it always amazes me when I see people neglect this opportunity to reinforce their brand.

The second category of people you dress for is joint venture partners. If you're looking to attract other people and other companies to align themselves with you and your image is forgettable, you will be forgotten.

People want to align themselves with people that are more successful than they are. Otherwise, what's the purpose of them aligning themselves with an external entity? I always want the people I do business with to look to me as the authority figure when it comes to knowledge, expertise, ability to execute, and power. Dressing the part is part of this persona.

The third category of people you dress for is your coworkers.

This is where the importance of building the culture of success within your organization comes in. When you're around people that are dressed well, you feel differently about your working environment. You feel differently about the work that you do. You feel differently about your team.

When you get everyone in your agency dressing for success, you see a huge difference in the energy and the overall vibe in your office. This is, and always has been, a big part of my company culture. When you walk into my office, there is an aura of success, largely due to the fact that my people are dressed well.

This brings me to the fourth person you dress for, which is the most important one: you dress for yourself.

When you're dressed to the nines and you know that your wardrobe is totally dialed in, you feel more powerful. You feel like a pro. In a world where most people are dressed casually (and look frumpy), when you're dressed impeccably, you have the edge, and you know it.

I know that when I'm dressed in a beautifully-tailored suit, I walk differently, I talk differently, I sit differently, I feel differently, and I act differently. As a result, I'm treated differently.

If you're a business owner or you're a key executive within the agency, I think it's absolutely imperative that you look successful and powerful at all times.

I've had so many people argue with me about this issue. They'll say things like, "I've been doing this for twenty-seven years, and I don't *need* to wear a suit and tie."

Hey, I agree with you. You don't *need* to wear a suit and tie, but I'll guarantee you this: when a guy like me walks into the room dressed for success, I'm going to steal the show, and you're going to lose the deal to me.

Part of the reason you got into this business in the first place was to have more control, right?

You didn't want a cubicle job. You wanted more control and more freedom, right? You feel like you've earned the right to not have to wear a suit and tie, and rightfully so. I totally agree with you. You've earned the right to not have to wear a suit.

But guess what. So have I, and I still wear a suit.

My business wardrobe (suits and ties) helps me make millions of dollars. It helps define who I am as a businessman and sends a message to people, reminding them of the level at which I do business. It sends a message to everyone I do business with, both overtly and covertly, both consciously and subconsciously.

It's part of my formula. It's part of my science. It's part of my brand.

If you want to be perceived as an icon in this business, trade in your khakis and your golf shirt for a navy blue suit.

Look at it this way: we don't *have* to wear suits. We *get* to wear suits.

Women's Attire

When it comes to women dressing for success, there are some basic rules that apply, as well.

A skirt suit always works better than a pants suit. Women tend to get upset when I say this. They'll say things like, "Darren, you don't understand how uncomfortable it is to wear panty hose every day," or,

"You don't understand that my legs get cold in the winter time, and I'm more comfortable in pants."

I'm not doubting that these statements are true. However, it is a proven fact that women wearing skirt suits are perceived as being much more powerful than women wearing pants suits. For example, Ivanka Trump (daughter of Donald Trump) always looks powerful and polished. Sure, she is a beautiful woman and has been raised in an environment that exudes wealth and power, but if you just look at how she dresses, she is practically always wearing a skirt (instead of pants) and is almost always in heels.

You don't have to be an ex-runway model for these rules to apply. I've seen heavier-set businesswomen look absolutely fabulous in a skirt suit and three-inch heels. This is a look that commands attention and respect.

In addition, businesswomen look more powerful with their hair up or back, as opposed to having their hair down. You may say, "But Ivanka Trump usually wears her hair down." Listen. Ivanka Trump *is* an ex-runway model. However, in my opinion, Ivanka Trump looks even more powerful as a businesswoman with her hair pulled back. Sure, long flowing locks can look very sexy on a woman, but in business, the goal is not to look sexy. The goal is to look powerful and knowledgeable. If you want to be taken seriously and you want to be perceived as a successful businessperson, it only makes sense to dress like one.

One of my favorite comedians did a standup act where he talked about how women dress. He posed a scenario where a woman is dressed extremely provocatively, and a man overtly hits on her. The woman is insulted and feels disrespected and says, "Wait a minute! Just because I'm dressed this way does *not* make me a whore!"

The comedian goes on to support the woman's statement, saying that men should not assume that a woman is promiscuous just because she is dressed in an overtly sexy manner.

But then he poses another fictitious scenario where he, the comedian, is dressed in a policeman uniform, and a woman approaches him saying, "Officer, officer, please help us!"

The comedian says, "Oh, just because I'm dressed this way does *not* make me a police officer!"

Of course, the audience erupted in laughter. He ends his story by addressing overtly sexy-dressed women by saying, "Fine, you are not a whore, but you *are* wearing a whore's uniform."

Of course, the audience roars with laughter once again. Now, why am I telling you about this comedian's stand up act?

Because it is directly applicable to the issue of dressing for success for both women and men. Right or wrong, people will make assumptions about you based on the way you present yourself, which includes the way you're dressed. It's only logical that if you want to be perceived as a successful businessperson that you should dress like a successful businessperson.

If you were going to play football, it would only be logical to wear football pads, a football helmet, and a football uniform. If you're going to do business, it would only be logical to wear a successful businessperson's uniform.

When you begin thinking about your business attire as a marketing tool to reinforce your brand, you will realize that it's equally (if not more) important than your website design, your business cards, and your brochures.

Chapter 8

How to Manage 1099 Independent Contractors

You Can't Make a 1099 Do Anything

Have you ever heard an insurance agency owner say this? Have you ever said this yourself? Let me tell you the real deal here.

It's true.

You can't force a 1099 independent contractor to do anything. However, you can inspire a 1099 independent contractor to do a lot. All of my producers are commission-only 1099 independent contractors. They don't have sales quotas. They aren't required to show up at a certain time. They have a lot of freedom.

How do I get them to produce? How is it that I can inspire them to make over one thousand cold-calls per week? Why are they so loyal to me? Why don't they leave me and go out on their own? How do I get them to work on straight commission, with no base salary?

These are questions that I get asked all the time.

Let me tell you something: it's not easy.

In the beginning, when I first started developing my agency, it was a major challenge. I remember the first sales crew I had. On the first day we officially opened our office, I reviewed the phone script with my producers, we identified the lists to call from, and I pulled the trigger on the starting gun.

Guess what happened.

No one picked up the phone to dial. No one did anything.

There I was, sitting in the middle of my sales floor with six producers, waiting for them to do something. They just sat there, fumbling their papers. One of them even whipped out a magazine and started reading it instead of making calls.

I was pissed.

Have you ever been in this situation? It's frustrating, isn't it?

One thing I've learned about effective leadership is that you cannot expect your people to do something that you're not modeling yourself. True leadership is about jumping into the trenches with your people and dialing alongside them. Leaders that don't lead by example are not true leaders.

There are five key rules when it comes to inspiring independent contractors that I'll discuss right now.

Rule #1: Lead By Example

A true leader sets the tone.

A true leader says, "Watch me do it, and do the same."

A true leader says, "Here, I'll do it *with* you."

Your people—especially the independent contractors—will respect you more when they see that you're practicing what you're preaching. They will become inspired to do the same.

You can't manage an independent contractor, but you can inspire an independent contractor. The only way people get inspired is when they see someone else accomplishing something that they want to accomplish, too. That's where Leading By Example comes in.

Your people are secretly asking themselves two simple things:

1.   Can I do this?

2.   Is it worth doing?

The first question cannot be answered with words. It must be proven with action, by showing them a live example. They must say to themselves, "I saw my leader do this firsthand, and it didn't seem that hard. If he can do it, then so can I."

Then you need to watch them do it, coaching them along the way. They'll wrap up the day saying, "I did it *with* my leader, and surprisingly, it wasn't that hard. I can do this!"

The second question is a question that rarely gets answered or illustrated, and it's why so many people quit the insurance business before they ever had a chance to be successful. Are you illustrating to your brand-new producer exactly what he or she gets if he or she dials the phone one thousand times per week?

If not, they're going to quit because question number two never got answered. What exactly are they going to get after one year of doing this grunt work? What about two years? What about five years? What about ten years?

When I bring on a brand-new producer, we walk them through an Electronic Truth Teller. This is a formula-driven spreadsheet that automatically calculates their commissions earned based on four variables:

1. Number of dials per hour

2. Number of dials per week

3. Booking percentage on the phone

4. Closing percentage in the field

I base this calculation assuming several constants, such as:

1. Average group size

2. Average premium per employee

3. Average employee participation

I then use these calculations to project my producers' income levels and extrapolate it out for years one, two, three, four, five, ten, and twenty.

Producers need to see real, hard numbers of where they'll be (income-wise) every step along the way, assuming they're doing the volume of activity they committed to. They are the ones that decide on their variables, including volume of activity and skill level acquired.

So under rule one—Lead By Example—you must show them that they can do it. You do this by modeling the activity for them first, followed by coaching them through the process while they do the exact same thing you just did.

This past week, I actually walked onto my sales floor and announced to my producers that I was going to make cold-calls with them for thirty minutes. You should have seen the looks on their faces, especially the new guys who have only been with my firm for a couple of weeks. I'm the president of the firm, but I hopped right in there with my guys.

As the president of my agency, I've gained my people's respect because they know I'm not above grinding it out in the trenches with them. They still couldn't believe that I would cold-call with them. I even announced that anyone that made more calls than I made in that thirty-minute period would get to go to lunch with me on Friday, my treat. You should have seen these guys blazing the phones.

I personally made thirty-one dials in that thirty minutes, but I had six of my guys beat me. These are the same guys that average thirty dials per hour, and in this thirty-minute period, they did more dials than they normally do in an entire hour.

Why? Because they got excited to see their leader jump in and do it with them.

In addition, you must show them exactly what they're going to get (commission-wise) if they diligently and consistently repeat this activity. This is where the Electronic Truth Teller comes into play. You can't just give them hypothetical approximations. Your income projections must be statistically based, not pie-in-the-sky hypotheticals.

So, without rule one, you will fail miserably at inspiring independent contractors. You'll live the majority of your business life frustrated and resentful, and it will be entirely your own fault.

But if you follow rule one to the tee, you'll build a super agency, make millions of dollars, and become the hero to your people.

Rule #2: Treat Them Like Partners, Not Employees

One of the biggest mistakes I see agency owners make regarding trying to manage independent contractors is that they treat them like employees. They're not your employees. If you treat them as such, it's like trying to herd cats. It's impossible.

Plus, they'll resent you for it because they (just like you) became an independent contractor because they didn't want to have to answer to a boss. You're not their boss, and if you want to argue that point, you'd better hope the Department Of Labor doesn't hear you arguing that point, or you'll be paying fines and penalties in the tens of thousands of dollars.

Even if you're paying for their overhead, you're still not their boss, so stop treating them as such.

What you are is a resource for them.

You've got to treat them as business partners. In a business where you both have skin in the game, which is what you have in a 1099-driven insurance agency, you are essentially partners in the deal. You've got to create an environment where it's easy for them to succeed because when they succeed, you succeed. The easier you make it for them to be successful, the more revenue they'll create, which ultimately is how you make a living as an agency owner.

I know a lot of people are surprised to hear me say things like this because I have a reputation for being a hard-ass. I'm not a hard-ass in the sense of being the boss. What I really am is a *clarifier*.

My job is to clarify to my producers what the end result will be based on the actions they're taking. In fact, in my quarterly planning sessions with them, I have them set their own goals. I don't have sales quotas in my agency. I let each producer tell me what their goals are, and I help them formulate an action plan around the goals that *they* set.

As great a motivator as I've been told that I am, the reality is that I've never been able to successfully guilt or convince someone into producing more, at least not long-term. I've heard all these self-proclaimed hard-asses talk about how they don't put up with below-average producers and how they come down hard on their people when they're not producing enough.

All you have to do is look at their producer retention, their agency's gross revenue, and the morale amongst their producers, and you'll see that their rule-by-the-iron-fist philosophy doesn't produce long-term agency success.

So, rule two is all about how you make your producers feel. Does that sound touchy-feely or what? I know, I know, but people, like it or not, *are* touchy-feely.

You need to be smart about how you treat your people. You'd be surprised at just how emotionally sensitive people are. The moment they feel that you're not on their side, they'll lose faith in you, and the more time that elapses where they feel like this, the more they will distance themselves from you. Ultimately, they will quit, and it will be your fault because you didn't lead them in the way that they needed you to.

I know what you're thinking right now. "Darren, this is bullshit. If they don't produce on their own, then it's their own fault. They're losers."

Hey, I know the feeling of frustration, probably more so than you do, and I have the same feelings that you do about this, believe me. Some of these people *are* losers, and many of them are total wusses compared to you. But here's the problem: if you're not able to get enough of these less-than-perfect people to produce business, feel good about you as a leader, feel good about your work environment, and if you can't make it easy for them to succeed, they will probably fail. As much as you know in your heart of hearts that it's not your fault, you have to ask yourself, "What will the end result be if this continues to happen with all of my producers?"

I'll tell you what happens. You'll have no producers left, no premiums generated, no long-term clients, and you'll be broke. How do you like these results?

You see, even if you're right, you're the one that ends up suffering. There aren't enough people in this world that are as talented, driven, passionate, and committed as you are. If you expect your producers to be all of these things at the same level you are, prepare to be disappointed.

The reality is, you should be thankful that they're not as driven as you are. If they were, they'd be your competitors, not producers at your agency. I make a lot of money from having a lot of people generating a little business. The cumulative value of the nonsuperstars is substantial, and if you're going to be a wise businessperson, then you'd better recognize and accept this fact.

Treat your producers like valued business partners, and jump in the trenches with them from time to time. This is how you win over their hearts, and they'll love you in the process.

Rule #3: Never Criticize

Have you ever criticized someone repeatedly and had your relationship with them get better? If you think you have, then you're totally ignorant. People do not respond well to criticism. They get defensive, and ultimately, they'll stop communicating with you. They will shut down and shut you out, resulting in them eventually leaving your organization.

So how do you get people to see the errors of their ways? You do this through a two-step process.

Step #1: Teach From Stage.

Teaching From Stage means that you teach certain principles in a group setting. When you're having a group staff meeting or when you're doing a producer training with multiple producers, you can criticize certain types of behavior without criticizing specific people. You can be a real hard-ass when it comes to criticizing behavior in a group setting, so for all you hard-asses out there, here's your chance. Be a total hard-ass when it comes to being adamant about how to run your business process and system, but do it from stage, and never, ever, ever criticize individual people.

So, step one is to criticize from stage, never one-on-one ... and ONLY criticize behavior, not people.

Step #2: Have Your Producers Self-Evaluate.

You should have quarterly, one-on-one progress meetings with your producers to discuss their performance, but here's the key:

Never criticize them.

All you want to do is review their numbers. That's why it's so important to track both activity results and production results. You've got to have a business system where you and your producers agree on a production goal.

Let them set their own goals when it comes to production. Remember, they're an independent contractor, which means they're technically in business for themselves. You are a resource for them to use. Once they tell you what *their* production goals are, you must design an action plan for them specific to the goals that they set for themselves.

In other words, in order for them to produce *x*, you must be able to tell them what level of activity (i.e., number of dials per week, number of appointments booked per month, etc.) they need to have in order to realistically reach their goal.

Now, the beauty of this goal setting process is that *they* are the ones that set the goal, not you. This means that they're taking ownership of their goal, and you are perceived as the mentor that is helping them attain that goal for *their* benefit, not yours.

Once you're in this role, your people will trust you more, leading them to be more loyal to you because they feel like you have their back. That's the type of relationship you want to develop with them. They should feel like they can come to you for anything. You're their coach, their confidant, and their leader.

Once these goals are set and the action plan is put in place, the one-on-one evaluation meeting is easy, which is where step two comes in. Have them tell you about their activity level and their production for the quarter (you should both be looking at the same production report print out), and ask them, "So how do you feel about your numbers?"

Notice, I didn't say, "How do you feel about how things are going." I specifically asked them how they feel about their numbers. Here's what happens:

If they're hitting their production goal, they get to tell you the good news. They get to tell you how well they're doing and how they're tracking perfectly. This is like a kid coming home with a report card to show his parents he's getting straight A's. It's a time of celebration and validation, and you get to congratulate them. They're seeking your approval, and you're giving it to them. This makes them feel proud and empowers them.

Now, if they're not hitting their numbers, they already know it. Having you scold them for it isn't going to help the cause. That's what's so great about consistent production reports. They can't escape the numbers, and the numbers don't lie.

When you review their production numbers together and you ask them how they feel about their numbers, they'll criticize themselves. They already know they're messing up. Just listen to them. They're probably embarrassed, and they're expecting you to criticize them, so they're already filled with anxiety.

When you don't criticize them and you just listen to them, they feel like you're being supportive, and therefore trust is built on a deeper level. You must keep the lines of communication open with your people, always.

When you let them self-evaluate, they're going to be harder on themselves than you were going to be on them, which is exactly what you want. They'll tell you what they're doing wrong activity-wise. This is an opportunity for you to help them redesign their action plan for the upcoming quarter. Again, they're empowered by this process because *they're* the ones that are setting their goals.

Now, when it comes to activity (or lack thereof), they're going to spill their guts to you and tell you how bad they're messing up and how they're going to work harder next quarter (in most cases). Just listen to them and be supportive because the reality is they're going to do whatever they're going to do, regardless. You might as well make them feel like you've got their back.

But here's where the real magic happens:

This type of one-on-one meeting ends with you asking them, "What part of your game do you feel you need the most help with?" Sometimes it's going to be closing. Sometimes it's going to be overcoming objections. Whatever the issue is, if you have a *System-*

Driven Business, you've taught a training session on this topic before. Instead of just giving them the answer, ask them if they remember the training you did on the topic.

Then ask them, "Okay, so how do *you* think you should handle this?"

Ask them, "What adjustments do *you* think you need to make?"

Ask them, "So what do *you* think is the best way is to handle this?"

In most cases, they already know the answer. If they come up blank, then just reteach that topic right there on the spot. If they do happen to give you the right answer, then just smile and say, "See, you already know the answer. Man, I've trained you well!" This should elicit a chuckle of relief from them.

The reason this type of teaching through discovery is so powerful is that it reinforces the fact that your business systems are *that* great. You've already taught them these principles because you foresaw these issues coming up before they actually came up. You're now perceived as a visionary because you've already been through the exact same thing they're going through, so you're relatable to them.

A great leader must be relatable to the common man. You must reinforce the fact that you are all-powerful while at the same time reminding your people that you started out just like them, so you get it. The minute your people feel that you've lost touch, they will lose respect for you, and they won't want to follow you into battle anymore. If they feel like you're right there in the trenches with them and like you understand what they're going through, they'll be loyal soldiers for you.

Now you've built trust with your people. They know what they're supposed to be doing. If they're not doing what they're supposed to be doing, they're aware of it, and they know you're aware of it. The question is, "How do you get people into action that aren't currently producing on a consistent basis?"

Obviously, ragging on them doesn't work, and using guilt never works long-term.

This leads us to rule four: Create Internal Jealousy within your agency.

Rule #4: Create Internal Jealousy

This probably sounds odd to you.

You must understand human behavioral patterns to really understand why this is so effective. Jealousy is one of the strongest emotions human beings have. Jealousy can drive us to do things that we normally wouldn't do. Jealous husbands have murdered their wives. Jealous wives have cut off their husbands' body parts (Remember Lorena Bobbitt?). Jealousy is a powerful emotion.

You need to use this human emotion to your advantage, especially when it comes to installing a new system or methodology into your agency.

In the past, whenever I used to come up with a new, brilliant idea, I would roll it out to all of my producers, and initially, only about 10–20 percent of them would embrace it and put it into action. The others would be very resistant to a new way of doing things.

Surprise, surprise.

That's just the way human beings are. It used to frustrate the hell out of me. So what did I do? I tried using guilt. I used to practically browbeat people into submission. I used to try to force them to do things my way.

Guess what the end result was.

I got people to do things my way for a week or two, and they begrudgingly did it because Darren said so, but after a couple of weeks, they went right back to doing things their old way. To make matters worse, not only did their actions not change permanently, but they also resented me for forcing them to do things my way.

Nobody won in this battle, especially not me.

I finally came up with a better strategy. I tapped into the power of creating Internal Jealousy. Here's how this strategy works:

Whenever I come up with a new, brilliant strategy, I roll it out to my two key producers. These guys are my testers. They understand that new ideas require testing, and quite frankly, these particular two guys love the process of trying new things.

If the test pilot bombs, no problem. No one knew it ever existed with the exception of me and my two testers. Most people don't understand the process of testing, and if they see two or more new ideas fail, they'll never be open to any new ideas ever again.

I see this happen in sales organizations all the time. After a series of failed new programs, whenever the organization launches their new *Best Idea Ever,* it's perceived as just another flavor-of-the-year gimmick. That's why you must test new ideas for at least four to six weeks before you roll them out to the masses.

Now, if your new strategy tests well, you're going to brag about your results to everyone. Talk about how much new business this new strategy is producing. Talk about how much money your key guys are making using this new strategy.

Here's what will happen:

Everyone else will get jealous. They'll want the same results your test pilot guys are getting, which means they'll be *begging* you for your new secret strategy. When this happens, you've created Internal Jealousy.

Once this happens, you won't need to force your people to do things your way. It's just the opposite. They'll be *begging* you to teach them your new way of doing things.

Mission accomplished.

You now have virtually 100 percent buy-in from your producers without even trying.

Last year, I developed a new selling process that I felt was going to revolutionize our production results. As always, I had my two test pilot producers (who, by the way, are two of my top producers) test this new strategy for a period of four months. I wanted to make sure that my hypothesis held true consistently over time, and I felt that four months was ample time to test this particular strategy.

In this four-month run, one of my test pilot producers, Scott, brought in thirty-seven new group cases. The other test pilot producer, George, brought in forty-two new group cases.

To give you an idea of how much of an increase this was, in the previous year, George increased his annual income by over $60,000 in that year by producing twenty-five new group cases in that year. In this four-month run, he brought in forty-two new group cases.

When I informed the rest of my producers what had happened, they went crazy. They were practically begging me to teach them what I had taught Scott and George.

Bingo.

I created Internal Jealousy, and everyone wanted in.

You see, this process makes you out to be the good guy. You're always going to have a handful of people opt out of the new deal, which is fine. The old deal was working just fine. Be supportive of them operating under the old way of doing things as long as they're producing.

Eventually, their jealousy of the superior results using the new strategy will override their resistance to change, and it will be a proven, indisputable fact that the new strategy is superior.

Either way, you (and everyone in your agency) will win, which is exactly what you want.

Always remember rule four. Using guilt and force repels your people away from you, creating animosity and poor results. Creating Internal Jealousy makes your people come to you, producing gratitude, loyalty, and ultimately, millions of dollars.

Rule #5: Become the Black Box

Agency owners are always worried about training their future competition, meaning they're always afraid of their top producers leaving them. Here's the deal:

When it comes to loyalty, most people have very short memory spans. As soon as a top producer feels that they can make more money without you, they will leave you.

Rare is the person that understands loyalty and remembers that they wouldn't be in this position today had it not been for your mentorship.

It would be nice if people understood this, but sadly, most do not. Don't fight it. It is what it is. So, how do you get your top producers to stick around? The answer is simple: prove to them that they'll make more money with you than they will on their own. This means that you have to continually deliver value to them.

This value can come in several different forms.

In my own agency, I have several resources that are irreplaceable. I've developed proprietary products with insurance carriers where I'm the only broker in the country that has access to them. That alone is huge and is based on the amount of volume I do with these carriers.

I also have tremendous carrier relationships that I've developed over the years. Once a year, I throw a relatively extravagant catered party at my home for carrier executives and the underwriters and customer service reps that work for the carriers. No other broker that I know of does this in my industry.

In an industry where brokers typically are entitlement-driven and always have their hand out, my agency's brand is completely the opposite. I want my carrier partners to know that I value them and appreciate their support. We usually have about seventy to ninety attendees, and the cost is substantial, but in business, you can't just look at the initial cost. You have to look at the return on the investment.

Sure I spend a lot of money on this event, but it sends a message to my carrier partners that I am different than all of these other entitlement-driven brokers.

When I go out to lunch or dinner with my carrier partners, I always attempt to pick up the bill. Sometimes, I get beat to the punch, but I want them to know that I don't expect to always be wined and dined. I know some brokers *never* pick up the bill because in their minds, it's not coming out of the person's personal pocket. The carrier rep is paying for the meal with their expense account.

That's not the point.

The point is that while every other broker is always going to the carriers with their hand out, expecting to be catered to, I'm branding myself as a partner as opposed to a client.

You may be saying, "They should be the ones paying because I'm their client." The truth of it is this:

If you unexpectedly pick up the bill, whereas every other broker is looked at as a freeloader, you've established your brand right there.

Let me give you an example of this.

I was speaking with a carrier executive once, and they were telling me about this broker that was always showing up for carrier events just to get the free lunch or dinner. For the sake of this story, we'll call this broker Bill. It became obvious to everyone that worked for this carrier that this broker was nothing more than a freeloader. Everyone that worked for this carrier nicknamed this broker "Free Meal Bill."

Think about this. Think about how this broker branded himself as a freeloader. Were the free meals really worth it?

Let's say he attended a carrier event once each month, and let's say the cost of these lunches served was $20. Maybe he saved $240 per year on lunches.

But what did it *cost* him?

His reputation.

That's why I make sure that I'm letting my carrier partners know that I view them as partners. While all of these other brokers want to be treated like princes, I get treated like a king. A wise king makes sure his people are taken care of, which ensures that he is loved, respected, and appreciated.

A wise star quarterback takes care of his linemen because without the protection of his linemen, he's going to get sacked a lot. If he doesn't have the protection of his linemen, he can't successfully pass the ball. If he can't pass the ball, not only will he not win the Super Bowl, but he'll also never reach superstar status as a quarterback.

I take care of my carrier people like a star quarterback takes care of his linemen. I need them as much as they need me. These carrier relations are part of what makes my agency so strong from a political standpoint, and my producers know this. They benefit from these relationships that I have created, and thus, they want to keep that benefit.

I've also developed joint ventures with other entities that deliver value to our clients, including a private-labeled payroll service, human resource consulting services, business succession planning services, and so on.

Another key component to the success of my producers revolves around Darren-Produced Content.

All of my producers know that I'm constantly upgrading our content, including sales scripts, sales strategies, marketing campaigns, and PowerPoint presentations. One of the most powerful forms of sales content I've developed over the past year is video communication.

All of our sales presentations are based around three-minute videos that explain concepts that we base our sale on. These videos not only communicate to the prospect why they should do business with our agency, but they also brand our agency. They're engineered in a way that best communicates our points in the most effective, efficient, and concise manner.

Within a year's time, these videos increased our overall closing percentage for the firm from 24 percent to 32 percent. This is part of what I call the Black Box. No one can duplicate the Black Box because no one understands how the Black Box works. This is the secret sauce of my agency.

There is no way someone could reproduce my videos because there is too much psychology and technology that goes into creating this type of content. My people know that I'm constantly developing new tools to make it easier for them to be more successful, which means that they'll make more money with me than they would on their own.

So, loyalty aside, from a purely selfish perspective, they'll stay with me because they know that they'll make more money with me. Here's an example of this:

I had a producer that I took from zero to making over $130,000 a year in less than three years, selling group health insurance exclusively. He went from driving a beat up, nine-year-old Acura with over 110,000 miles on it to driving a 7-Series BMW (a $94,000 car). He got greedy and felt that he could make more money if he left me and went out on his own.

Four years later, two of my top producers ran into him at a party. Both of my producers are now driving $100,000 cars and live in $1 million homes, and they've been with me for seven years now. When the ex-producer left me four years ago, he was renting an apartment, living with his sister as his roommate, driving that 7-Series BMW. Today, he's still renting that same apartment with his sister, but now he's driving a BMW 3 series (a huge downgrade).

Now, as much as it pleasures my ego to know that this clown is making less money without me and that his income and lifestyle have actually gone backwards since he left me four years ago, the reality is, we both lost the war on this one.

He lost the ability to make tons of money with me, and I lost a solid producer. That's why I'm so adamant about what I'm teaching you in this chapter. When I look back at why this producer left, it was really my fault. I forced him to do things my way and made him feel ashamed and guilty when he didn't follow my lead. I criticized him more than I encouraged him. I didn't keep the lines of communication open between the two of us. I didn't make him feel like I had his back.

He felt disempowered working at my agency, and thus, he left.

You could argue that I was right, and I would agree with you. I was in the right, but the end result is that we both lost. The bottom line is that I didn't follow rules one through four, because at that time, I hadn't developed these rules yet.

A lot of times, we business owners let our egos get the best of us. Sure, we may be right, but being right doesn't always make us the most money. Being smart and making calculated business decisions is better than being right, especially when it comes to dealing with our people.

At that time, I hadn't created a strong enough Black Box, which made this ex-producer think he could do better without me. Had my Black Box been fully developed, he would have realized that he could make more money working with me than he could going out on his own. Creating the Black Box gives you control because your people are relying on your secret sauce to ensure their success, and without you, the Black Box doesn't exist.

Chapter 9

Managing Expectations

Managing Expectations

The insurance industry as a whole has a terrible producer retention rate. Typically, more than 90 percent of the people that enter this business will quit within the first year. Why is that? I'll tell you why that is.

People quit this industry because they didn't experience success soon enough, so they never saw the light at the end of the tunnel. I've realized that the key to retaining straight-commissioned producers is getting them to experience success firsthand as soon as possible. In my agency, my brand-new producers are successfully booking cold appointments within their first or second day.

Our system produces this success, and this immediate experiential success is what makes that new producer actually show up the next day.

If they come back the next day, they'll stick around for a week.

If they stick around for a week, they'll stick around for a month.

If they continue to experience success, they'll stick around for a year.

If they continue to experience success, they'll stick around for another year.

By then, it's too late to back out because they're making more than double what their friends make, and they're successful. They have the income to back it up. They're lifers now.

That's how we build our people's careers.

In terms of managing expectations, we let them know what to expect with no fluff whatsoever. I tell them,

"You're going to be a workaholic for the first two years. You won't even see your first commission check until your fourth month. After nine months, you'll be making about

$700 a month. You'll be working ten to twelve hour days, and your friends and your family will think you've joined a cult. They won't understand why you're working so hard for so little pay. What they don't understand is the power of renewal commissions. Once you hit the twelve-month mark, you should be making about $1,800 a month. You're not rich, but at least you can pay your bills. But the next year, you'll bring in more clients, which add to the cumulative commission accumulation. You should be making about $5,000 a month at this point. After your third year, you should be making $8,000–$9,000 a month. And after your fifth year with us, you should be making $150,000–$200,000 per year. If you want a cubicle job with a base salary and you want to go to Taco Tuesdays with your friends every week, if you want to do as little work as possible and have a salary cap of $40,000 per year, then go work at a bank or something. Go sit in a cubicle. But if you really want to go for the big time and make over a quarter of a million dollars per year, and you're willing to work hard for it, this may be the place for you."

Don't Compare This to a Job

This is not a job. This is a career.

Sure, you could go and get a cubicle job and make more money in your first year, sitting in a cubicle, but that's all you'll ever be: a cubicle worker.

Think about how long you went to college for. It was probably four or five years. You didn't make any money going to college full-time. In fact, *you* paid *them*.

So, why did you go to college?

You went to college because you perceived that it was a good investment of your time, that it would ultimately lead to a better career.

Deciding to enter this business is similar to that mindset. Sure, you don't make a lot in your first year, but as you accumulate your client base, you'll make more and more over time. Starting a career in this industry as a commission-based producer is an investment that will pay huge dividends over time.

You need to drill this into your producers' heads from the moment they walk into their first interview with you. You're looking for people that understand this concept and are of this mindset. When you speak to this demographic, you won't have the kind of producer turnover you've been having because you're only attracting the right kind of producers.

Another challenge you'll have with new producers is that they get discouraged very easily. It's your job to encourage them and provide clarity for them. Let them know that this is not an overnight process. For example, think about something you're good at. The first time you tried it, were you good at it? Probably not. You had to practice it, over and over, and your skill probably wasn't developed overnight. It took time.

Today, I was coaching a cold-calling session in Dublin, Ohio, with about forty employee benefits brokers. One of them was a bit discouraged. He told me, "I've made a bunch of calls, and I haven't even come close to booking an appointment yet."

"Okay," I said, "Let's see how many calls you've made so far."

"Fourteen," he replied.

Fourteen? Under my cold-calling system, you're going to have a decision-maker contact rate of 11 percent. That means 89 percent of all the calls you make is going to end up in a voicemail box because the business owner isn't available. So, if you made fourteen calls, the most business owners you could expect to talk to is one or two. Under my system, the average booking percentage is 14 percent. What's 14 percent of one? It's less than one!

So here's this guy that's all bent out of shape because he hasn't booked an appointment yet. Well, based on understanding the expected statistical results, he shouldn't have expected to book an appointment yet. Once I shared this with him, you should have seen the look on his face. He was totally relieved.

Here he was, feeling like a total failure, but when I clarified his expectations, he realized that it was too early in the game to evaluate his results. He had only made fourteen calls. You can't even begin to evaluate cold-calling results on less than four thousand dials, minimum. When people let their emotions get wrapped up in cold-calling results, they avoid the process, and you and I both know what happens when a producer avoids the prospecting process.

Lack of prospecting is the single biggest reason people fail.

You need to constantly reinforce that this is a numbers game, and if you have clearly defined (and statistically proven) expectations, your producers will be far less susceptible to negative emotions and realize that for every one thousand calls they make, they're only really expected to book about fourteen appointments.

If they make one thousand calls, at a 10 percent contact rate, they would have talked to one hundred decision-makers.

If they book 14 percent of those one hundred decision-makers, that's fourteen appointments.

Now, there's no way to know when those fourteen appointments are going to surface. They could all come in the beginning, they could be evenly spread out over the one thousand dials, or they could all come at the end. The point is that it doesn't matter.

This is a numbers game, and in a numbers game, you have to play by the law of large numbers. You cannot evaluate the viability of this process after only a handful of calls. The minimum number of calls you can make and begin to evaluate these statistics is four thousand, and even then, it still isn't enough to determine a true run rate. If you look at a grouping of ten thousand calls, you'll see that my projections—using my scripts, my coaching, and my systems—will produce exactly what I projected.

This volume of activity reminds me of the Sex Story.

The Sex Story

One day, there was a man standing on the street corner. Whenever a woman walked by him, he said, "Hey, do you want to have sex with me?"

Woman after woman walked by him, rejecting his proposition over and over. Finally, one woman was so offended by his proposition, she stopped and said to the man, "I'm deeply offended that you would say such a thing!"

She then slapped him across the face and said, "You must get a lot of slaps!"

The man replied, "Yeah, but I also get a lot of sex!"

The Moral of the Sex Story

I hope that this little tongue-in-cheek story didn't offend you. It's just so analogous to what we do in sales. We propose an idea, and most of the time, that idea gets rejected. However, over time, we find enough people that like our proposition, and so the rejection is worth it.

The point is that in the game of prospecting, volume always produces results. The reason volume always produces results is that there is a segment of the population that wants what you have. It may not be the majority, but in our business, it's large enough to make millions of dollars.

There are business owners out there that would love to work with someone like you, that would value the service that you provide. The goal is not to convince some knucklehead that they should dump their current broker and work with you. The goal is to find the right prospect, at the right time, that wants what you have.

Just like the man standing on the corner in the story above, there's a certain percentage of the population that wanted what he was offering. Maybe his target market just had their boyfriends cheat on them, and this guy provided an easy way for them to seek revenge. Maybe his takers were going through some exploratory sexual liberation phase and saw it as an opportunity for a discrete sexual encounter.

Or maybe they were just horny.

The point is that through prospecting enough women, he found the ones that wanted what he was offering. It certainly wasn't the majority of women by any means, but by doing a large volume of prospecting, he got a larger volume of takers. It was more of a right prospect, right timing issue as opposed to trying to sweep each individual woman off her feet.

In sales, you're looking for the easy ones. Again, I hope this example doesn't offend you, as that is never my goal. My goal is to get you to see that statistically, if you contact enough prospects, you'll find the ones that just so happen to want what you're offering.

There are tons of predestined no's, and for those predestined no's, there isn't a damn thing you could have possibly said to get them to say yes. This is almost always the majority.

Who cares?

You're not looking to close the majority. You're looking to pick up the small handful of prospects that have some level of dissatisfaction with their current situation. If that percentage is 20 percent of the population, that means that in order to get one new client, you have to get in front of five prospects.

It's really quite simple.

If you have a lack of prospecting volume, you tend to focus on the no's.

If you're doing a ton of prospecting volume, you tend to focus on the yes's.

Sure, rejection may make you feel uncomfortable, but being comfortable is overrated, especially if you want to be successful.

Being Comfortable Is Overrated

Success is not about being comfortable. If you want to be comfortable, go sit in a lounge chair, sip on some hot cocoa, and get a foot massage.

Success is about discovering what works and doing that thing over and over, regardless of how you emotionally feel about doing it.

It's about results, not comfort. Ironically, when you get really great results, the discomfort begins to fade away. Massive success makes you very comfortable.

Focus on the comfort of success through results, not the comfort of staying in your little emotional comfort zone bubble.

As a leader of people, it's important that you let your people know that when you first started out, you were scared and uncomfortable, too. This is part of being relatable. Your people are going to be uncomfortable, just like you were. Your job is not to make them feel more comfortable.

Your job is to let them know that it's okay to be uncomfortable in the beginning and that doing anything new, and outside of their comfort zone is going to be a little scary. However, show them results and give them an opportunity to experience success, and watch that uncomfortable feeling vanish right before your very eyes.

Chapter 10

Successful People

Successful People

I've made it a lifelong goal to study successful people.
I love talking to successful people, hearing stories of their humble beginnings and how they've transformed their bleak situations into millionaire lifestyles.

It's a passion of mine to better understand what makes successful people successful. Obviously, there are certain characteristics that these people have, things like tenacity, competitiveness, dedication, integrity, and the list goes on, but I'm always looking for the formula.

Why are some people so driven? What drives them?

In dealing with some incredibly successful people in my life, one common element that they have all had was a sense of purpose. They had a level of crystal clarity as to why they were doing what they were doing. They had a big-picture vision.

Typically, most successful, driven entrepreneurs have a big, compelling reason why. There's a reason why they work so hard, and usually this reason is more complex than the simple desire to make more money.

In almost every case, these successful people are fighters. They're survivors of great adversities. Most of the incredibly successful people I've met have an equally incredible story to tell regarding their struggles during their rise to the top.

Many of them have either lost everything or came close to losing everything or have gotten knocked down at some point in their career or their personal life. But they had something inside of them, a competitive, never-say-die spirit, that made them fight through the adversity and soar out of the pit of death like a phoenix rising.

A good example of this is my good friend Dave Rice.

Dave and I grew up together in Long Beach, California. Dave, by his own definition, grew up poor. Dave's parents didn't have cars. They rode bicycles. When they could afford it, sometimes they'd take the bus. Their house had no telephone, and they often borrowed the neighbor's hose for running water when their utilities were turned off. Sometimes, there was no food in the house.

When we were in high school, his parents decided they couldn't make it financially in California, and they moved to Colorado. Dave decided to stay in California, so at age seventeen, during his senior year in high school, he dropped out and got a full-time job to support himself. Dave worked full-time, but he always had some sort of entrepreneur-type of project he was working on.

At age eighteen, Dave was managing six frozen yogurt stores and several one-hour photo labs, but his eyes were set on larger goals.

At age nineteen, Dave decided his next venture would be to own a nightclub, and he set out to build a business plan. Within a few months, he had solicited enough investors who believed in his vision to move forward. Dave maintained majority ownership and had invested none of his own money, mostly because he didn't have any.

To everyone's amazement, he was able to lease a large building and secure permits. The club had a capacity of nearly twelve hundred people and had one area for hip-hop, one for punk rock, and one for gothic/industrial music fans.

The nightclub was called Toe Jam, and he got the hottest DJ's and bands from all around to perform at his club. Many superstar acts performed and frequented the club, including Snoop Dogg, No Doubt, The Offspring, and Green Day, and the members of Sublime were near permanent fixtures.

The club was usually packed, but a number of factors including Dave's lack of business experience, very high overhead, and some internal theft from hardcore gang members meant that Dave and the club were barely surviving.

To give you an idea of how little profit the club was generating him, at the end of each night, Dave would lock the doors, turn on the lights, and look for loose change on the floor. He'd use that change to go across the street and buy $0.99 hamburgers from a local burger joint. That was his dinner. To keep expenses low, he lived in some office space in the attic of the club.

Given the nature of the club's clients, there were regular fights and even some shootings, including a gun battle between two rival gangs that yielded nearly a hundred rounds being fired. This happened right in front of the club.

One night, an off-duty police officer ended up shooting a gang member right in front of the club after a standoff. This was the end of Toe Jam.

With no business and no job, Dave had to figure out what his next move was going to be.

Dave applied for jobs at McDonalds, Warehouse Records, and just about anywhere he found a help-wanted sign. He also applied for a job with a company called Pro Sound, which was the DJ equipment company he had bought his sound and lighting equipment from for his nightclub.

He was fortunate that his relationship with the sound and lighting supplier was strong, and he received a sales clerk position. While most of his friends were out partying, Dave worked and worked and worked.

He was constantly looking for ways to develop better business solutions, and he came up with the idea of marketing this company's products through mail-order catalogs, which was something brand-new for this industry. Obviously, this was before the internet.

This innovative idea took this company to new level, and in a relatively short amount of time, Dave became the President of Pro Sound. Dave grew Pro Sound into a multi-million dollar company.

Earning a name for himself in the industry, Dave went on to lead several multi-billion dollar corporations. Dave served as CEO of several well-known brands, including Cerwin Vega.

Fifteen years later, Dave went back to Pro Sound (the company that gave him his first sales job), and he put a deal together and bought the company. Dave would consider himself a serial entrepreneur, and he continues to develop new business ventures. I can't wait to see what he does next. I have an enormous amount of respect for Dave and what he has accomplished.

I have another good friend of mine that started out his real estate development career around the same time I started my insurance agency. Roston Thomas was in the business of buying homes and apartment buildings, fixing them up, and flipping them. Not only would he negotiate the deal and put the deal together himself, but he would also do a lot of the manual labor on the renovation himself, along with his construction crew.

Roston's strategy was to work a regular job for about six months and save as much cash as he could. He would be making a $70,000 salary, but he'd take the bus to work and live extremely frugally.

Once he accumulated enough cash, he'd quit his job, take his savings, and pour all of his money into buying a small fourplex apartment building or a fixer-upper house. He'd bring his crew in and remodel the project with the intention of increasing its value, then sell it for a handsome profit.

Roston would keep repeating this process. Buy. Remodel. Sell. Get a job. Live like a rat and save as much cash as possible. Pour all of his cash into a new project. Remodel. Sell. Repeat.

Often times, Roston would work so late and have to get up so early in the morning to work on the project that he would just sleep in a sleeping bag on the concrete floor of his jobsite. Roston would spend every last penny he had to put these deals together. Needless to say, he didn't have a problem with taking big risks. He'd do whatever it took to be successful.

I remember during this time in our careers that I'd occasionally drive up to Los Angeles and meet him at whatever property he was working on. We'd talk about how our businesses were coming along. If you were to ask Roston how our conversations went, he'd probably tell you that I encouraged him and motivated him to keep pressing on. In reality, he was the one that was giving me the encouragement that I needed.

We'd talk about how successful we were going to be one day. We'd talk about the big dreams we both had. I think it's important, especially in the beginning of your journey towards building your empire, to surround yourself with likeminded people.

Roston always used to say to me, "D, we ain't ever gonna give up, right? We ain't ever gonna quit, right?"

I would reply, "That's right, man. We ain't ever gonna quit."

Roston was a great friend to me during this rough time, and he continues to be a very dear friend to me. He will never truly know just how much his encouragement kept me going, emotionally. It was a rough time for both of us during these early years, cash flow-wise, fatigue-wise, and sanity-wise.

But we made the commitment to each other and to ourselves, that we would under no circumstances ever quit.

Keep grinding it out. All day. Every day. No excuses.

Here we are seven years later, and Roston has made several millions of dollars and helped his family in ways that most sons and brothers could only dream of. He has been incredibly generous to his family with his success.

I have a tremendous amount of respect for Roston, and I have appreciated his friendship and his encouragement over the years. He has been a great friend to me.

I could go on and on about people of this caliber, people that have a burning desire to succeed, who will stop at nothing to accomplish that which they set out to accomplish.

So what's the common thread that connects people at this level?

I believe that they view their pursuit of excellence as if it were a reflection of their entire character. They have to succeed because if they give up and quit, that would be in direct conflict with who they are as a person and who they aspire to be as a winner.

As I'm writing this final chapter, I'm on a flight back home to Orange County, California, from a speaking engagement in Omaha, Nebraska.

At the end of my speaking engagement today, I asked the people to talk about why they chose their profession. One man in the back of the room had just begun his career, and his response to my question was incredibly powerful.

He talked about how he wants to give his family a better life than he had growing up. I would say most people that want to be financially successful are driven by wanting to provide a better life for their families, but that's not what stuck with me.

What really got to me about what this gentleman said was that he talked about how he wants to prove to all the little boys that are growing up in the ghetto (where he grew up) that they can accomplish their dreams if they put their minds to it and work really hard.

Think about this.

He's taking on the responsibility of leaving a legacy behind, not only for his own family, but for the community he grew up in.

He wants to inspire people.

He wants to give these young boys hope.

He wants to empower people.

You see, in my opinion, there is no greater gift you can give someone than the power of believing in oneself.

I don't care how independent and driven you are, we all need to have someone tell us, "I believe in you." Empowering someone by encouraging them to have the audacity to dream big is a very special gift. It's the gift that I try to give people every day of my life.

It's the reason I wrote this book.

It's the reason I do what I do.

I had a very unrealistic dream, that one day I would build the most successful insurance agency the industry had ever seen.

Most people laughed at me.

Many people tried to talk me out of it.

Very few people were encouraging or positive.

But you see, that's where you find out what you're really made of. Will you listen to these people and let them talk you into giving up on your dream, or will you persevere and keep fighting until you accomplish your dream?

Character isn't built on the mountain tops. Character is built in the valleys when you've been knocked down.

You see, in my opinion, success isn't necessarily defined by what you accomplish in life. It's defined by what you overcome in life. It's about how many times you get back up after you've been knocked down. It's about developing character.

In my own life, I've tried to focus on developing character more so than developing riches. Character is the only thing you take with you when you die. Character is everlasting.

When I think of all the times that people tried to get me to quit, all the times when I felt like giving up, all the times I felt like I might not ever make it, and I look at the lifestyle that I have today, I think to myself, "Thank God I didn't quit."

You see, what makes *your* dream so special is that often times, you're the only one that can see it. You'll have people tell you all the time to be more realistic. You'll have people that will put your dream down and sometimes even put *you* down.

Hold on to your dream, and don't let anyone steal it from you. Hold it close to your heart, and never, never, never give up on your dream. Sure, you're going to doubt yourself from time to time. Sure, you're going to be afraid from time to time.

It's nothing to be ashamed of.

Courage is not the *absence* of fear.

Courage is what you do *in spite* of the fear.

Be courageous.

Be the hero to your family.

And when all of those negative people out there try to talk you out of pursuing your dream, just remember that the greatest pleasure in life is accomplishing things that other people said you could not do.

About the Author

Darren Sugiyama was born in Long Beach, California, and attended Loyola Marymount University, where he earned his Bachelor's Degree in Sociology. Darren was the team captain of the varsity baseball team at LMU and was selected as an all-conference player in the 1991–1992 season.

Upon graduation, Mr. Sugiyama returned to his home town of Long Beach, working with at-risk youths as Director of the LBCGP Gang Prevention Program. He went on to further his philanthropic work through counseling inmates at Halawa Prison and incarcerated youths at the Honolulu Detention Home in Hawaii.

During his counseling work in Hawaii, he continued his education at the University of Hawaii at Manoa and earned a Master's Degree in Multicultural Education.

Mr. Sugiyama eventually returned to his love for business and became the Western Regional Sales Director for the $200 million denim company Mudd Jeans.

In 2003, Mr. Sugiyama founded Apex Outsourcing Insurance Services and has led Apex to being the most sought-after firm in Southern California.

By 2009, after only seven years in the insurance industry, Apex was writing over $37 million in annual premiums, almost solely focusing on small employer groups of 10–20 employees.

Mr. Sugiyama currently sits on Kaiser Permanente's esteemed Broker Advisory Board as well as Colonial Life Insurance's Broker Advisory Board and has been invited to speak at exclusive roundtable planning meetings by Aetna, Blue Cross, and Blue Shield.

In addition to serving as the President of Apex, Mr. Sugiyama also founded Ontogeny Consulting, a business development firm that consults businesses on developing a stronger company brand, sales and marketing training, and streamlining operations of high-growth businesses.

Despite Mr. Sugiyama's busy schedule, he still finds time to give back to the community, talking with and encouraging young people to think about their life choices and their future careers.

For more information about Mr. Sugiyama, visit his personal website at www.DarrenSugiyama.com.

30017740R00080